The Seafood Book

A COMPLETE COOK'S GUIDE TO PREPARING AND COOKING FISH AND SHELLFISH

SHIRLEY ROSS

The Seafood Book

A COMPLETE COOK'S GUIDE TO PREPARING AND COOKING FISH AND SHELLFISH

Illustrations by
Beth Cannon

McGRAW-HILL BOOK COMPANY

New York St. Louis San Francisco Bogotá Düsseldorf
Madrid Mexico Montreal Panama Paris
São Paulo Tokyo Toronto

Book design by Clint Anglin.

1234567890DODO 876543210

First Paperback edition, 1980

Library of Congress Cataloging in Publication Data

Ross, Shirley.
The seafood book.
1. Cookery (Fish)   2. Cookery (Shellfish)
I. Title.
TX747.R67   1978   641.6'9   77-26176
ISBN   0-07-053881-6
        0-07-053889-1 (Paperback)

To Bill, Jean, and Pepper

Contents

[Recipes are found throughout the book—in various chapters and under each fish in the Fish Dictionary, Part V. Refer to the Index for specific recipes.]

PART V: FISH DICTIONARY

Introduction

Fish is one of the most delicate and most rewarding foods you can cook and eat. There are over 30,000 species of bony fish—more than in any other class of vertebrate animals—all of which are edible. Approximately 250 species of edible fish and shellfish are available commercially in the United States. Fishery products offer more variety than any other food group and are available fresh, frozen, canned, dried, salted, smoked, and in many convenience forms. These cold-blooded, aquatic creatures are also interesting in their own right, and it is only fitting that they be properly (if generally) introduced before becoming the object of a hungry eye.

There are three classes of fish: the *Agnatha* (such as lampreys and hagfish), primitive, jawless, and ugly too; the *Chondrichthyes*, or cartilagenous fish (sharks, skates, rays)—with weak underdeveloped jaws and paired fins—almost all of which are saltwater species; and the *Osteichthyes*, or bony fish, the most highly developed group with skeletons formed of bone, including many saltwater species and all freshwater species in North America.

Most fish in our inland waters are exclusively freshwater inhabitants. However certain fish, described as *anadromous*, return to fresh water to spawn after spending most of their lives in the sea. Pacific salmon, shad, smelt, and some trout are examples. Other fish described as *catadromous*, live in freshwater streams and lakes and descend each year to the sea to lay their eggs. The American eel is the only common catadromous species in the U.S. Some freshwater species often move out of brackish water or sea water at the mouths of rivers, although never venturing far into the sea.

What is it like to be a typical fish? Do fish hear or have a sense of smell? Do they distinguish colors? Can fish feel pain? Do fish sleep? There are no set answers to these questions because fish can differ radically.

Most fish, despite the absence of external ears, have an acute sense of hearing. Fish have internal ears imbedded in the skull bones that are as complex a mechanism as the human ear. Because sound generally travels through water faster than in air, fish do not require external ears to catch sound waves or ear drums to carry the sound. When sound waves vibrate through the water and strike the flesh and bone of a fish's head, the waves are relayed to the inner ear which then transmits them to the brain. Fish have a sixth sense that is a combination of hearing and touch. A lateral line on the fish (a stripe, not always visible) extends from the gill cover down each side to the tail. The area along this line contains a complex system of sensitive nerves that picks up low-frequency vibrations not caught by the human ear. This complex of nerves *feels* sounds as represented by changes in water pressure, sounds as discreet as a bug bouncing on the surface of the water.

Many fish have a keen sense of smell, especially the predators such as sharks who depend on it to locate their food. Fish with an acute sense of smell are equipped with a kind of tongue—whiskerlike barbels around the mouth—or taste buds located in the body, that enable the fish to distinguish sour, salty, bitter, and other taste sensations. The only taste they cannot distinguish is sweet because few things taste sweet underwater.

Fish can also distinguish colors, some more sensitively than others.

Fish can feel pain, so say the scientists, but not as intensely as humans or animals, and the sensation is quickly forgotten. Experiments in this area continue because the results have been rather inconclusive, and the debate is ongoing.

Fish don't sleep, but they do hibernate. Hibernation is common with fish in the temperate zones where lakes and streams freeze. Unlike warm-blooded animals whose temperatures remain constant, regardless of external temperatures, cold-blooded fish must adjust to the temperature of their environment. In winter, when lakes and streams are sealed with ice, the metabolism of the fish slows down to the point where they can live on stored energy and do not require external nourishment to maintain life processes. However walleyes, crappies, perch, and other game fish remain fairly active throughout part of the winter season.

The outermost surface of the skin on a fish is composed of living cells. Whereas human skin is covered with several protective layers of transparent, hardened dead cells, the living skin cells of fish can be exposed because these cells live in a liquid medium. The slimy or mucous covering on the skin that sticks to your hands when you handle a fish is simply a useful coating that serves several purposes: as an excellent lubricant to permit fish to slide through water with a minimum of friction; as a protection from bacteria, fungus, and other parasites; as a watertight shield, vital because the skin of most fish is a semipermeable membrane—without this waterproof coating, fish would become waterlogged!

All fish are protected by armor in the form of scales, although this armor may not always be visible. A fish scale, when viewed under a microscope, reveals the age, rate of growth, and other details of its life. A scale is similar to a ring in a tree. A particular species of fish can be identified from its scales.

Fish continue to grow throughout their life span, but, like a tree, their rate of growth slows down with age. The average maximum life span of freshwater fish, according to available evidence, is from eight to ten years, with a small number of fish reaching that ripe old age.

As food, fish is an excellent source of high-quality protein, vitamins, and minerals. It is especially rich in essential amino acids—the vital protein components that cannot be manufactured by the body from materials in foods. An average serving of seafood provides nearly all of one day's requirement of animal protein. The flesh of fish contains little or no connective tissue and is therefore very digestible (from 85 to 90 percent) and easily assimilated by the human body.

The B vitamins (thiamine, riboflavin, niacin, nicotinic acid, vitamin B_6, vitamin B_{12}, pantothenic acid) are especially abundant in fish. Some fish contain vitamins C and D. These vitamins are important for the normal functioning of nerve tissues and other parts of the human body. Minerals (calcium, potassium, phosphorous, copper, iron, manganese, magnesium, cobalt) are found in rich quantities in all fish products. Minerals are essential for the proper metabolism of body tissues and the maintenance of sound teeth and bones. Saltwater fish contain from 50 to 200 times as much iodine as is found in other foods. The sodium content of both freshwater and saltwater fish is very low.

The calorie content of fish and shellfish is very low, especially if cooked simply, without rich sauces, and by methods other than frying. The fat content of fish varies according to species. For salmon and mackerel, it can be as much as 20 to 25 percent, making it high in energy value. In the cod family, the fat content can be less than 1 percent.

One of the main concerns of modern living is a healthy and nutritious diet. We're constantly bombarded with information on how and why we should exercise and eat well. In spite of this, we continue to consume meat in ever-increasing quantities. Also, fast foods, whether in restaurant chains or in supermarkets, constitute an obstacle course few of us have managed to avoid.

Why not try fish? It's low in calories, high in energy, it's good for you. We live in a land graced by shoreline, spotted by lakes, and criss-crossed by rivers. If there is one natural, national food we all can eat and enjoy, it's fish. Here in this book is something good to do with every fish you are likely to meet. I hope this book will give the novice and the experienced cook alike a sense of both the simplicity and variety of fish cookery, as well as a lot of good eating.

PART ONE
Buying Fish

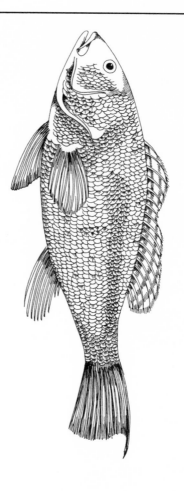

CHAPTER ONE

Buying Fresh Fish

Fish are both superior in quality and less expensive when abundant; many varieties of fish are more abundant during certain seasons of the year. The most economical fish to buy are usually the less popular species which are nevertheless satisfying in taste.

The first consideration in buying fish is whether you want fish that is lean or fat and oily in character.

LEAN FISH (Up to 5 percent fat)
Although lean fish do not have as high a nutritive value as fat or oily fish, they have a delicate flavor, are very digestible, and are superb with sauces. This category includes the medium-fat fish (fat content from 2 to 5 percent). Medium-fat fish are more fatty during certain seasons of the year. Blood streaks, which appear as red or dark lines in the flesh, are rare in lean fish.

Lean fish include:

bass (all)	fluke
brook trout	grouper (saltwater)
chub	haddock
cod	halibut
crappie	mullet
cusk	perch (all)
flounder	

pompano	snook
salmon	sole
(landlocked)	sunfish
sea trout	swordfish
(weakfish)	turbot
shark	whitefish
skate	

FAT OR OILY FISH (Over 5 percent fat)
Fat or oily fish have a high nutritive value and energy-producing capacity. They are less digestible than lean fish and have a strong flavor. Their flesh is not white but of a dark tint: Salmon and trout are a pale pink; mackerel, bluefish, and most tuna fish are pink or grayish in color.

Other fat or oily fish include:

barracuda	pickerel
carp	pike
catfish	pollack
cod	porgy
drum	red snapper
eels	smelt
grouper	sheepshead
grunion	striped bass
hake	sturgeon
herring	sunfish (ocean)

HOW MUCH TO BUY

A fish dealer will prepare your fish in any way you desire. Or, you can buy a whole fish and prepare it yourself. Fresh fish is available by the pound in any of the following market forms or cuts:

Whole: A small or medium-sized fish that comes directly from the water and keeps fresher at the dealer's without dressing. Before cooking, it must be scaled and the entrails removed. The head, tail, and fins are also usually removed, although this is not essential. The fish may then be cooked whole, stuffed, filleted, or, if big enough, cut into steaks or chunks.
   Buy 1 pound per person.

Drawn: A whole fish with only the entrails removed.
   Buy 1 pound per person.

Dressed or Pan Dressed: A fish that has been scaled and the entrails removed. The head, tail, and fins are usually removed as well. Depending upon the size of the fish, it can be cooked whole, filleted, or in steaks or chunks. Small fish prepared in this manner are called ''pan dressed'' and are ready to cook as purchased. Large fish are usually marketed in steaks or chunks.
   Buy ½ pound per person.

Filleted: Fillets are the sides of a fish cut lengthwise away from the backbone. They are practically boneless and ready to cook as purchased.
   Buy ⅓ to ½ pound per person.

Single Fillets: A fillet cut from the side of a meaty fish. The plumpness and size of the fish determine the thickness and weight of the fillet, which can range from a few ounces to several pounds. Although some fillets have skin, the majority are skinless. Single fillets are readily available in markets.

Butterfly Fillets: Two sides of the fish cut lengthwise away from the backbone and held together by the uncut flesh and skin of the stomach.

Steaks: Cross sections ⅝- to 1-inch thick (or thicker, on occasion) of a large, dressed fish. A cross section of the backbone runs through the center of the steak. Steaks are ready to cook as purchased.
   Buy ⅓ to ½ pound per person.

Chunks: Very thick cross sections of a large, dressed fish with the backbone running through the center. Chunks are ready to cook as purchased.
   Buy ⅓ to ½ pound per person.

Sticks: Pieces of fish cut lengthwise or crosswise into equal-size portions from fillets or steaks.
   Buy ⅓ pound per person.

CHARACTERISTICS OF FRESH FISH

Fresh fish, whole or dressed, have the following characteristics:

Skin: When fish is first caught, the markings and colorings have an iridescent quality that begins to fade as soon as the fish is taken from the water. The skin should be shiny and the color unfaded.

Scales: The scales should appear bright and shiny and adhere compactly to the skin.

Flesh: The flesh should be firm and, when depressed, spring back with elasticity. The flesh should cling closely to the bones without separation. This means the fish is fresh and has been carefully handled. When a fish seems limp, the fibers have relaxed and the fish is not fresh.

Odor: The smell of newly caught fish is fresh and mild. The odor should never be disagreeable. As a fish ages, the fishy odor becomes more pronounced.

Gills: The gills should be reddish in color and entirely free from slime. With age, the gills turn light pink, then gray, and finally a greenish brown color.

Eyes: The eyes of a fresh fish should bulge and be bright, transparent, and full. The mucus covering the eye should be clear. When a fish is stale, the eyes often turn pinkish and cloudy, taking on a sunken appearance.

Vent: The vent of a fresh fish protrudes and is pink.

Fillets: The flesh should be firm-textured with the edges free of any browning or drying. The cut surface should be moist.

Wrapping: If you purchase your fish from a supermarket, the wrapping should be secure around the fish, with little or no air space between the fish and the wrapping. The material used to wrap the fish must be moisture- and vapor-proof.

STORING FRESH
FISH IN THE REFRIGERATOR

Fish is extremely perishable and must be wrapped and stored properly as soon as it is brought from the store. If left unwrapped, fish will dry out and lose quality within an hour. Also, the cold air of the refrigerator can transfer fish odors to other foods. Before wrapping remove any congealed blood that might be hidden under the backbone. Scrape it off with a sharp knife and wipe the fish clean with absorbent paper towels.

Wrap the fish as airtight as possible. For large fish, use aluminum foil or freezer paper. Wrap small pieces of fish in foil or freezer paper, or put into a storage container and cover tightly.

Fish must be kept in the coldest part of the refrigerator at 34° to 40°F to maintain freshness and quality. If properly wrapped and kept at this temperature, the fish will keep for three days (but should be used sooner). Some seafood will lose flavor in 16 hours, even if kept on ice. Don't keep fish lying in water; this will cause it to lose its freshness.

Any leftover cooked fish should be immediately stored in a tightly covered container.

FREEZING FRESH AND COOKED FISH

Whole fish must be cleaned and either left whole or cut into fillets or steaks before freezing. (See Chapter 5.)

Lean fish (see beginning of this chapter) can be kept frozen for six months to one year and still taste delicious. Trim away any blood streaks so they don't become rancid. Scrape the inside of the fish with a sharp knife and wipe it clean with absorbent paper towels.

Lean fish with a mild flavor can be dipped into a brine solution, consisting of ⅔ cup salt to 1 gallon of water. Dip for 30 seconds at most. This treatment reduces drip after gutting and holds the flavor.

Fatty fish (see beginning of this chapter) can be successfully frozen for about three months. Their freezer life is short due to the oils in the flesh that easily become rancid. Mullet and mackerel become rancid within two weeks and are not successfully frozen.

Fish that are fatty and strong-flavored should not be brined. To lessen the chance of flavor change during storage, dip fatty fish into an ascorbic acid solution, made of 2 teaspoons crystalline ascorbic acid available in drugstores, dissolved in 4 cups of cold water, for 20 seconds.

Cooked fish must be properly wrapped and not kept frozen longer than three months.

Scaleless fish, catfish, and cusk must be skinned before freezing. Otherwise, the skin absorbs moisture from the flesh which will become tough and spongy (see Skinning, Chapter 7).

WRAPPING FOR THE FREEZER

Each piece of fish must be wrapped carefully in a moisture/vapor-proof material such as aluminium foil, polyethylene, freezer paper, plastic bags, or plastic wrap to ensure airtightness and to avoid freezer burn (spots that have dried out). Freezer burn is not harmful, but the dried areas will be tough and tasteless. If there is one dried spot, you can be pretty sure that the fish has lost flavor.

If you're wrapping more than one steak or fillet in a package, place pieces of freezer paper between each piece for easy separation later. Use a piece of wrap large enough to have considerable overlap on all sides of the fish. Bring the sides of the wrap together above the fish and fold down in small folds until snug against the fish, pressing out all air. Seal the ends securely with tape so the package does not become loose in the freezer.

Label the package directly with a felt-tip pen or grease pencil, or use a separate piece of paper and tape it on the package. Indicate the type of fish, date frozen, and the weight or number of servings.

Fish must be frozen at 0°F or below. Any variance in temperature results in chemical changes, causing the fish to lose color, flavor, texture, and nutritional value.

CHAPTER TWO

Buying Frozen Fish

Most varieties of fish are available in frozen form. Frozen fish products are usually packed and frozen during the seasons of abundance and held in cold storage at 0°F or below. They remain in good condition for a comparatively long period until distribution, making possible the availability of a wide variety of fish throughout the year.

Frozen fish products compare favorably with fresh fish in nutrition and appearance, and may be used and prepared in the same manner as fresh fish.

HOW MUCH TO BUY

Frozen fish are marketed by the pound in the same cuts as fresh fish (see Chapter 1), as well as in a variety of precooked forms.

Fried Fish Sticks, Fried Fish Portions, and Raw, Breaded Fish Portions:
These forms are cut from frozen fish blocks, coated with a batter, and breaded. Fried fish sticks and fried fish portions are cooked partially, then packaged and frozen.

Raw, breaded portions and fried portions are at least ⅜-inch thick, weigh more than 1½ ounces, and must contain not less than 65 to 75 percent fish.

Fried fish sticks are at least ⅜-inch thick and weigh up to 1½ ounces and must contain not less than 60 percent fish.

All of the above are ready to heat and serve as purchased, according to instructions on the package.

Buy ⅓ pound per person.

FISH STICKS

1 package (10-ounce) frozen fish sticks
¼ cup almonds, chopped and toasted: use a frying pan to brown nuts without oil, constantly stirring to avoid burning
1 cup shredded cheese, Cheddar or Parmesan

2 tablespoons onion, minced
¼ cup milk
½ cup sweet pickle, chopped
2 tablespoons buttered dry bread crumbs

Preheat oven at 425°F. Arrange fish sticks in a shallow baking dish. Mix remaining ingredients, except bread crumbs. Spoon over fish. Top with bread crumbs. Heat in oven for 15 to 20 minutes. Serves 4.

CHARACTERISTICS OF GOOD FROZEN FISH

Most deterioration in quality of frozen fish is prevented by keeping at 0°F or below without any thawing and refreezing.

Frozen fish of good quality have the following characteristics:

Flesh: The fish should be frozen solid when purchased. The flesh should not be discolored. Lean fish (see list in Chapter 1) have whiter flesh than fat or oily fish. Salmon and trout are pale pink; mackerel, bluefish, and most tuna are pink or grayish. There should be no signs of freezer burn (dried spots). Areas with freezer burn will be tough and tasteless and usually indicate that the quality of the whole piece has deteriorated.

Odor: Frozen fish should have little if any odor. Strong odor means poor quality.

Wrapping: Most frozen fish or pieces are wrapped individually in packages of various weights. The wrapping should be made of moisture/vapor-proof material and should be secure around the fish, with little or no air space between fish and wrapping.

If the package has a swollen appearance, the fish was probably thawed, partially or completely, and refrozen. If there is a bulge at one end of the package, the fish was thawed, the liquid moved to one end, and the package refrozen. In these cases, the fish will be tasteless or will taste spoiled.

Keep frozen fish, packaged in original wrapping, in the freezing unit or frozen-food compartment of the refrigerator at a temperature of 0°F until ready to use. If the temperature varies, the color, flavor, and texture—as well as the nutritional value of the fish—will be lost through chemical changes. To enjoy the best flavor of the fish, the time of storage should be short. Do not allow the fish to thaw and then refreeze it. Thawed fish must be used at once.

THAWING FROZEN FISH

Breaded fish portions and fish sticks should not be thawed before cooking. Other fish must be cooked soon after it is thawed. Schedule the thawing so the thawed fish does not remain uncooked for more than one day. Put the package of frozen fish into the refrigerator and allow about 24 hours for thawing per one pound package. Fish should never be thawed at room temperature or in warm water: it will become soggy and shapeless.

If it is necessary to thaw a piece of fish quickly, put the individual package, or packages, into a plastic bag. Seal it tightly and immerse it in cold water. Allow one to two hours for a one pound package to thaw completely. *Do not refreeze!*

For broiling, boiling, or baking, the fish does not have to be thawed completely. Simply increase the cooking time.

For frying, breading, or stuffing, fish must be thawed completely. Stuffing a partially frozen fish can be very difficult. Frying frozen fish in hot oil is dangerous because the oil will spatter. Also, the temperature will drop below the proper frying level and the fish will either brown on the outside before the center is cooked or will absorb the oil, resulting in a greasy, fat-soaked dish.

Baking a piece of fish taken directly from the freezer is fine. The fish should be wrapped in foil. Make sure there are no holes in the foil before putting it into the oven to bake. After a half hour, open the foil and add any seasoning, vegetables, or sauces. Close the foil and finish baking (see Baking, Chapter 9).

CHAPTER THREE

Buying Canned Fish

Tuna, mackerel, salmon, and sardines are the most common and abundant canned fish. There is, however, a wide variety of other canned fish available, as well as many specialty items.

Canned fish should be stored in a cool, dry place for no longer than a year.

TUNA

Many species of fish are marketed as tuna. The Atlantic Coast has the little tuna. The Pacific catch includes blackfin, bluefin, and skipjack. Albacore of the Pacific is the only tuna permitted to be labeled "white meat tuna." The others are darker in color and labeled "light meat tuna."

Tuna is available in three different styles of pack, which refer to the size of the pieces in the can, not the quality.

Fancy or Solid: Contains three or four large pieces, generally packed in oil, although it can also be packed in water. It is used for fancy salads and is the most expensive canned tuna.

Chunk: Tuna in smaller chunks. Moderately priced.

Flaked or Grated: Tuna cut up into small pieces and packed in oil. Priced lower than the others.

Canned tuna can be purchased in cans of about 3½, 6, 7, 9¼, and 13 ounces.

MACKEREL

Chunks—15-ounce cans; fillets—4-ounce cans.

SALMON

There are five distinct species of salmon canned on the Pacific Coast. The meat varies in color, texture, and flavor. The deeper red in color have more oil content and are priced higher.

Canned salmon is sold by name. The grades of salmon in descending order according to price are:

red or sockeye;
chinook or king salmon;
medium red, coho, or silver salmon;
pink salmon;
chum or keta salmon.

Salmon can be purchased in can sizes of 3¾, 7¾, and 16 ounces.

SARDINES

Available in can sizes of 3¾ or 4 and 16 ounces, packed in oil, mustard sauce, or tomato sauce.

CHAPTER FOUR

Buying Shellfish

Oysters, mussels, clams, and scallops are bivalve mollusks, having two shells that open and close. The snail is a one-valve mollusk. Crustacea are shellfish, whose bodies are covered with a thin, removable shell or crust. These include shrimp, prawns, crayfish, crabs, and lobsters.

Shellfish can be purchased in many forms. There are obvious ways to identify fresh shellfish, making their selection easier than purchasing fresh fish.

For the correct amounts to purchase, check under individual varieties in Chapter 5.

ALIVE AND FRESH

Live clams, mussels, and oysters feel heavy when held in the hand. Their shells should be tightly closed or should close immediately when handled. Otherwise they are dead and should be rejected.

Crabs and lobsters are easily recognized as live by the brisk movements of their head parts and claws. Fresh crabs, lobsters, and crayfish must be purchased and cooked alive with the exception of spiny lobsters, whose tails are marketed in the fresh-frozen state. When dead, they become soft and lose their best qualities.

All live shellfish must be eaten soon after purchase or frozen.

FRESH AND UNCOOKED

Most, though not all, species of shrimp and prawns are sold headless. They should be firm to the touch and greenish in color, although the color can vary in some species.

SHUCKED

Shucked shellfish are removed from the shell. All shellfish are available in this form.

Deep-sea scallops (large) and bay scallops (small) can be purchased in the shucked form only. They should be firm and white in appearance.

Oysters, crayfish, shrimp, and spiny lobsters freshly shucked are available frozen all year long. Thaw in the refrigerator, allowing 24 hours to defrost. Do not refreeze.

COOKED MEAT

Prawns, shrimp, lobster, and crabs are available shucked, cooked, and ready-to-eat. Crab and lobster meat are sold in containers weighing one pound or less. Prawns and shrimp are sold loose in desired amounts.

Shrimp, prawns, lobsters, and hard-shelled crabs are available cooked in the shell.

Always select those that have been kept on ice and have no strong odor.

Crab meat is available in several forms:

- All white meat in a lump form. This meat is from the large muscles.
- All white flake meat. This is the rest of the body meat.
- A combination of the above forms.

The claw meat of the blue crab has a brown coloring on the outside; rock crab is brown; the dungeness crab, or Pacific Coast crab, has a red coloring, and body meat and claw meat are packed together.

CANNED

All shellfish, both foreign and domestic species, are available canned and ready-to-eat. They have been shucked, peeled, and cooked—whole or minced—and usually packed in a salt solution.

SMOKED

Smoked whole and sliced oysters in cans are available in gourmet shops.

FREEZING SHELLFISH

Methods of freezing shellfish vary according to the specific fish.

Shucked oysters, clams, scallops: Pack the shellfish in freezer containers, leaving ½ to 1 inch of space between the fish and the top of the container to allow for expansion. Mark the container with the name of the fish, date frozen, and quantity. Always use within a three-month period.

Crabs and Lobsters: Cook before freezing (see Chapter 16 and the Fish Dictionary). Place in a freezer container, freezer wrap, or aluminum foil. Mark the container or wrapping with name, date frozen, and quantity. Store no longer than one month.

Shrimp: Shrimp is best frozen in the shell. Place the shrimp loose on the freezer shelf until frozen. Then wrap in moisture/vapor-proof material or freezer containers. This method of freezing allows easy removal of the amount of frozen shrimp you want to use. After removal of desired portion, make sure the package is resealed tightly, eliminating as much air as possible. Uncooked frozen shrimp keep for about ten months; cooked shrimp about five months.

PART TWO

Preparing Fish for Cooking

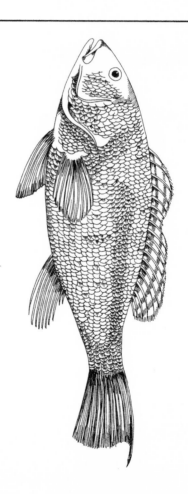

CHAPTER FIVE

Cleaning and Dressing

SCALING
GUTTING
DRAWING

Look at the following illustration of the fish. Note the names of the different parts. Knowing the parts of the fish will help in understanding the process of cleaning a fresh fish.

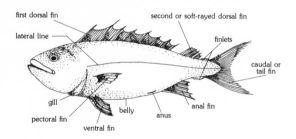

BASIC EQUIPMENT
FOR CLEANING FISH

*   A thin, sharp knife with a stiff blade, or a fillet knife with a 6-inch blade
*   A fish scaler, or a spoon or dull knife
*   A pair of pliers
*   A good working area
*   Newspapers

The size of the fish you purchase determines the type of preparation necessary. Large fish (over 25 inches) are delicious as steaks. Medium fish (15 to 24 inches) can be left whole for baking, filleted, or butterfly-filleted. Small fish or panfish (less than 12 inches) are excellent left whole and pan fried or broiled. Some of these small fish do not have to be scaled (stream trout, saltwater pompano. Check individual fish in the Fish Dictionary, Part V). Scaleless fish, particularly catfish and cusk, must be skinned before cooking or freezing or the skin will absorb moisture from the flesh and become tough and spongy (see Skinning, Chapter 7).

TO CLEAN YOUR FISH

1. First, wash the fish quickly in a solution of 1 tablespoon salt to 1 quart of cold water.

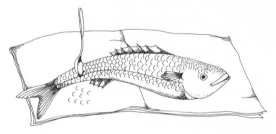

2. Scales are removed more easily from a wet fish. Place the fish on top of several sheets of newspaper on a solid working counter. As your debris collects, throw away layers of paper. Place stomach of the fish toward you. Hold the head firmly with one hand. With the other hand, hold the fish scaler vertically and remove the scales with short, quick movements, beginning at the

tail and scrape against the grain toward the head. Be sure to remove all scales around the anal and dorsal fins, base of the head, and throat. They are easily missed unless you are careful.

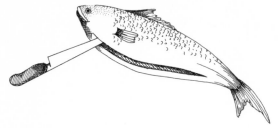

3. Removing the internal organs (viscera) and gills is called gutting or drawing. For both large and small fish, slit open the entire length of the belly from the vent (anus) to the head. For large fish, first cut the stomach between the gills, then remove the internal organs. A white secretion from the male reproductive glands, called milt, is considered a delicacy, especially in herring, shad, and smelt. It has a mild sweet flavor and does not have to be removed unless desired. Make sure all blood streaks are removed, using the point of a knife to remove any viscera that are attached.

If you plan to cook the fish whole, remove the gills. Small fish gills are removed easily by simply pulling them out with your fingers. Large fish gills must be pulled out with pliers toward the vent. The viscera are usually attached to the gills, if they haven't already been removed.

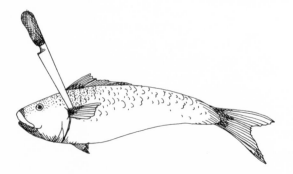

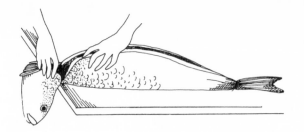

4. Next, to remove the head and the pectoral fin, use a sharp knife to sever the throat underneath the pectoral fin, moving the gills toward the head and cutting through right behind them. The backbone can be broken by a twisting motion. For a large fish, hang the head over a solid edge of the counter and snap the bone by bending the head down sharply. Cut through any flesh that holds the head to the body.

5. To remove the tail, slice straight through it.

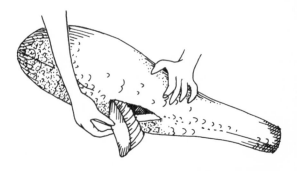

6. Next, remove the dorsal fin, the fin located on the back of the fish. If the fish is to be cooked whole, the dorsal and ventral fins can be left on and removed easily after cooking. This fin and its root bones are easily removed by slicing the flesh on each side of the fin the length of the fin and close to it. Hold the fin and pull it quickly toward the head. Then, remove the ventral fin (on the underside of the fish toward the back) in the same manner; there is no other method to remove the small root bones.

Do not use shears to cut off fins! Many

fish dealers shear fins, leaving the root bones in rather than removing them properly.

7. Finally, remove any remaining entrails by washing the fish in cold water.

8. Remove the skin, if necessary (see Skinning, Chapter 7).

The fish is now dressed, ready to be prepared in another form, or pan dressed and ready for cooking. After preparing fish, it must be immediately cooked or stored (see Storing Fresh Fish, Chapter 1).

CLEANING AND SHUCKING SHELLFISH
See individual shellfish and crustacea in the Fish Dictionary.

CHAPTER SIX

Filleting

Filleting a fish means cutting the sides of the whole fish lengthwise from the backbone. It is not necessary to clean the fish before filleting unless the skin is to be left on while cooking. In this case, only scaling the fish is necessary. Look up your particular fish in the Fish Dictionary to make sure the skin is edible. To remove the skin, see Chapter 7.

TO FILLET

1. On a hard surface place whole fish on its side with the dorsal fin facing you.

2. Insert a thin, very sharp knife diagonally behind the head and the pectoral fin. Cut down to the backbone, but not through it. Remember that the backbone runs through the middle of the fish, not along the top.

3. Turn the knife, keeping it flat, and slide the knife along the rib cage with a sawing motion toward the tail to the very end of the rib cage, lifting the flesh from the rib cage and backbone with the other hand.

4. Insert the knife flat from the backbone to the anus and remove the flesh from the bones by cutting gently along the backbone.

5. Lift the fillet in one piece. Use the tip of the knife to cut away any rib bones that have adhered to the fillet.

6. Turn the fish over and repeat the preceding five steps.

7. Cut through any skin connecting the two fillets. Discard the rest of the fish, unless you want to use it for stock (see Stock Recipes in Chapter 18).

FILLETING FLATFISH

Flatfish must be skinned before filleting (see Skinning Flatfish, Chapter 7). Underneath the skin is an indentation in the fish, separating a double set of fillets, two on the dark side and two on the light side. With a very sharp knife, cut through the flesh on both sides of the spine. Slip the knife under the fillet close to the bone and cut each fillet loose from the backbone, cutting toward the edge of the fish, not the tail.

FILLETING A LARGE FISH

The problem with filleting a large fish is that your knife will not be long enough to cut through the width of the fish.

Follow the steps for filleting of fish discussed previously in this chapter. For large fish, cut along the dorsal surface all the way to the tail. Lift the fillet by the edge, and with a sawing motion cut the flesh away from the backbone.

Repeat this procedure until you have reached the skin on the stomach. Cut through the skin and your fillet will be intact. Turn the fish over and repeat on the other side.

Leave the fillets large for broiling or baking. Cut them in half to serve.

THE DOUBLE OR BUTTERFLY FILLET

Double fillets can be done only with fish that have edible skin. Check the Fish Dictionary for the fish you intend to use.

Follow the procedure for filleting discussed previously in this chapter, but *be careful not to cut through the skin of the stomach.* This skin holds the two fillets together, making the double fillet.

- Double fillets are excellent for cooking

over a campfire (see Charcoal Broiling with a Grill, Chapter 11).
- Place a stuffing on top of one fillet. Fold the other fillet over it. Secure the edges with toothpicks and bake.

BONING FILLETS OF SHAD

Special care is necessary when boning shad because of its very bony structure. Fillet the fish according to the instructions in this chapter.

Lay the fillet with the skin side down on the working surface. The extra bones in a shad fillet run in two rows down the length of the fillet, approximately 1 inch on either side of the center.

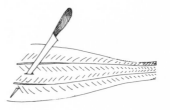

Make a lengthwise cut ½ inch from the center of the fillet on each side of the center. Work the point of the knife underneath the bone and pry it up enough to get a grip on it with your fingers. Pull it gently and, at the same time, work the bone out of the fillet with the point of the knife. Do the same on the other side of the center.

MAKING STOCK FROM SCRAPS

After filleting a fish, there is no need to throw away the scraps, which can supply enough fish meat and flavors to make stocks for soups and chowders.

1. To separate fish meat from bones, poach the skeleton for 1 minute in 4 cups of boiling water to which 1 teaspoon salt and ¼ cup vinegar have been added.

2. Drain, saving the liquid. Allow the bones and fish to cool. Use a fork to separate

the meat from the bones. Put the bones back into the liquid and simmer for 15 minutes.

3. Strain, saving the liquid but discarding the residue. Return the pieces of fish to the liquid. The liquid can be frozen in airtight containers for future use. It will keep for six months.

CHAPTER SEVEN

Skinning

Skin adds to the flavor of some species of fish. In others, it imparts a strong, disagreeable taste. With those fish that aren't too bland, removing the skin results in a slightly milder flavor.

Skinned fillets are usually more desirable. However, if you prefer broiling fillets, the skin will retain the juices while the fillet cooks.

TO SKIN

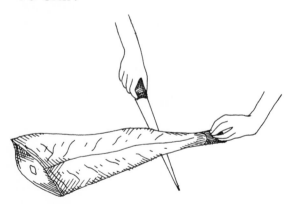

1. Place the fillet skin side down on a hard cutting surface, the tail toward you. Hold the tail tightly.
2. Hold a sharp, pointed knife almost flat, with the edge pointing slightly downward, and cut through the flesh at the tail end to the skin.

3. Flatten the knife against the skin. Pull the skin with one hand as you cut toward the head, using a sawing motion with the knife in the other hand, to about ½ inch from the end of the fillet, separating the skin from the flesh. Always exert more pressure in pulling the skin than in the motion used in cutting with the knife.
4. The fillet will detach from the skin in one piece. Wipe the skinned fillet with a damp paper towel (do not hold in running water).

SKINNING SCALELESS FISH

Catfish, cusk, and other scaleless fish have tough skin that must be removed before the fish is dressed. The skin is thin and slippery and easily removed. However, the removal process is different from that for fish with scales:

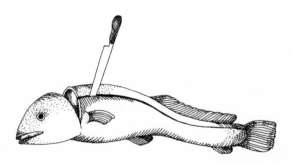

1. With a sharp knife, cut the flesh behind the head from one side to the other across the top.

2. Next, bend the head down to break the bone. Make a cut on the fish the length of the back up to the crosswise cut.

3. Holding the backbone and rib cage firmly, slowly pull the head toward the tail; the skin should peel from the flesh in one piece. If the skin tears, grip the skin and pull again.

4. Finally, remove the head and dress the fish.

If the skin is to be removed *after* cooking, it can be done successfully with the sharp point of a small knife.

SKINNING FLATFISH

1. Cut through the skin above the tail and peel it back until there is enough to grasp with the hand (about ½ to 1 inch).

2. Hold the tail flat with one hand and pull the skin toward the head with the other.

CHAPTER EIGHT

Steaking

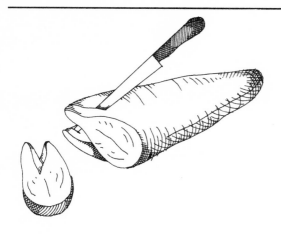

Halibut, salmon, swordfish, king mackerel, and other large fish are especially good as steaks:

1. Dress the fish.
2. Place the fish on its side on a hard surface with the back facing you.

3. Beginning at the nape, behind the head, slice equal cross-section slices straight through the backbone about 1-inch thick (or thicker, if you like). Thinner slices are good for fast cooking; thicker slices for slower cooking when you use sauces. However, don't make the steak too thick or the outside will tend to overcook.

If you meet resistance when slicing through the bone, use a cleaver to hit the blade of the knife or use a frozen-food knife to sever the bone. Then continue to cut through the rest of the flesh.

4. As you reach the tail, the steaks become smaller. Use the tail section for fillets (see Filleting, Chapter 6), or broil or bake it in one piece.

5. The skin is usually left on the steaks. However, check the Fish Dictionary to make sure the fish you are steaking has edible skin.

PART THREE

Cooking Fish

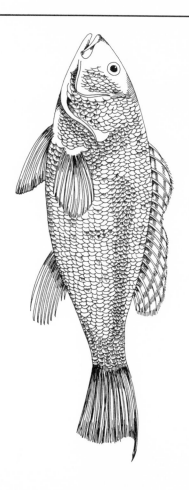

Fish is an exceptionally delicious food when it is properly and imaginatively cooked. The distinctive flavor of a particular fish is brought out by the cooking process. Fish does not require tenderizing; cooking makes the connective tissue soft enough to eat and the proteins easily digestible.

Fish cooked without sauces should be basted with butter, olive oil—or a combination of these—or citrus juices.

A variety of flavoring ingredients that are readily absorbed by the fish may be added during the cooking process, such as parsley, paprika, garlic powder, dry mustard, sweet or sour cream, wine, fresh lemon. Herbs—such as oregano, thyme, tarragon, fennel, chives, and dill—can be varied to create different dishes from the same species of fish.

Before you cook fish, it is a good idea to have all required ingredients on hand. The speed and gentleness with which you handle and prepare seafood determine how delicious it will be. Fish breaks up easily during cooking and should be handled only when necessary.

How can you tell when fish is cooked? Raw fish is watery with a translucent appearance. During the cooking process, the juices turn a milky color and the flesh becomes opaque and white. This change is easily discernible: when the thickest part of the fish is transformed in this manner, the fish is completely cooked. The flesh should flake easily when a fork is inserted into the thickest part of the fish. Cooking fish too long or at too high a temperature toughens, dries, and shrinks it; overcooking also destroys the delicious flavor.

Most fish can be cooked as you please— baked, broiled, fried, and so on. Most recipes can be used with all similar types of fish. However, an allowance must be made for the fat content of the fish during the cooking process.

HOW TO REMOVE
BONE AFTER COOKING

1. First, lay the fish flat on a cutting board or plate.
2. Next, remove head and tail.
3. With a table knife, gently make a cut lengthwise, about 1 inch from the upper edge of the fish, cutting into the fish just to the backbone.
4. Next, slice knife along the top of the backbone while gently lifting the top section of flesh away from the backbone. Place this section on a plate. Repeat with the bottom section.
5. Carefully slide the knife under the backbone while lifting it away from the fish. Use a fork to help the procedure. Discard the backbone.
6. Gently replace the two pieces of fish in their original position. Head and tail may also be replaced, if desired.

HOW TO KEEP FISH ODOR
OFF HANDS AND UTENSILS

Run hands in cold water before handling raw fish. After cooking, rub hands with moistened salt, rinse in hot water, and wash with soap.

To clean utensils, first soak or rinse utensils in hot salt water and then wash in soapy water.

CHAPTER NINE

Baking

Baking, or cooking by dry heat, is the easiest way to cook fish. The secret to perfect baked fish is to bake for a short period of time in a 350°F oven. This method keeps flavor and moistness intact, keeps the fish tender, and prevents drying. Any size or style of fresh-water or saltwater fish can be baked; whole (2 to 8 pounders are best), fillets, steaks, or drawn. Frozen fish can be baked as is if the cooking time is increased to allow for thawing during the baking process and if the recipe doesn't call for stuffing or rolling (see Thawing Frozen Fish, Chapter 2).

TO BAKE

1. Either clean and dress the fish yourself or have your fish dealer do it. Make sure it is scaled well and that the bloodline located under the backbone is completely removed. Check the Fish Dictionary to be sure the skin is edible since some fish have to be skinned before or after cooking.

2. If you are baking the fish whole, the head can remain. The meat in the head in most species is tastier than the rest of the body and the cheeks of some fish, salmon for example, are a delicacy. Leaving the head intact also seals in juices as well as being decorative.

3. If you're stuffing a whole fish or fillets, never overstuff: the stuffing will swell and break the delicate cooked flesh of the fish. When you're preparing the fish to be stuffed, make sure the belly of the fish is not cut all the way to the tail, but only from the vent (anal opening) to the head. This leaves enough connective tissue to hold the stuffing intact. After stuffing, close the cavity or the sides of fillets with skewers or toothpicks, or lace it with thread.

4. Use a shallow baking pan. Oil the bottom well, or butter brown paper, waxed paper, or aluminum foil and place it on the bottom of the pan. Arrange a bed of vegetables, cut thick, and dotted with butter or oil on the bottom of the pan. Carrots, onions, or celery, will enhance the flavor of the fish. Discard them after cooking.

5. Pat the fish dry and place it on the bed of vegetables.

6. Fish must be kept moist during baking. If you're not using a sauce, baste with melted butter or oil; butter and oil equally combined; or strips of bacon or salt pork laid on top of the fish; fish stock or white wine. Or marinate fish in wine vinegar mixed with herbs or French dressing for one hour before baking and use the marinade to baste, or use fruit juices.

During baking, it is necessary to baste

every 15 minutes. Smaller portions of fish (fillets or steaks) need either to be basted more often or, after placing the basting ingredients on the fish, wrapped in aluminum foil to prevent drying.

7. Place the baking pan on the center shelf of the oven.

8. Doneness of fish depends on various factors: the thickness and texture of the fish; if the fish was cooked frozen or just after purchase; the thermostats in ovens, for example. Cooking time varies from 30 minutes for a 2-pound fish to 90 minutes for an 8-pound fish. It normally takes 20 to 30 minutes to cook a fish under 2 pounds.

Estimating Cooking Time:

Dressed
2 to 3 pounds   350°F oven   30 to 60 minutes

Pan-dressed
3 pounds   350°F oven   25 to 30 minutes

Fillets or Steaks
2 pounds   350°F oven   15 to 25 minutes

Frozen Fish Portions and Sticks
400°F oven   15 to 20 minutes
(unless package specifies differently)

Alternate method:

Measure thickness of the fish and cook 10 minutes per inch—or, if frozen, 20 minutes per inch—in a 450°F oven:

Whole fish, fillets, steaks	Measure the depth at the thickest part when laid on the side.
Stuffed fish	Measure after stuffing
Rolled fillets	Measure after rolling
Foil-wrapped	Add 5 minutes for foil to heat; 10 minutes if fish is frozen

---

After two-thirds of the approximate cooking time, test for doneness by inserting a fork into the back of the head (the thickest portion); the meat, if done, should flake to the bone and not show any pink.

9. Serve immediately after cooking. Fish has a tendency to become soggy if allowed to stand after cooking.

BAKING FISH IN FOIL

---

1 fillet (white-fleshed)
1 12"-square aluminum foil
¼ cup onion, minced
¼ cup celery, minced

¼ cup carrots, thinly sliced crosswise
Salt and pepper to taste
⅓ cup fish stock or bottled clam juice
2 tablespoons dry white wine

Place onion and celery on foil and put fillet on top. Turn up edges of foil. Add remaining ingredients. Fold edges together and seal tightly. Place foil in a shallow pan. Bake in preheated 400°F oven for 25 minutes or until done. Serves 1.

BAKED FILLETS OR STEAKS

2 pounds fish fillets or steaks, fresh or
   frozen
2 tablespoons melted butter or oil
2 tablespoons lemon juice

1 teaspoon salt
½ teaspoon paprika
   Dash pepper

Thaw fish if frozen. Cut fish into 4 portions and place in a single layer, skin side down, in a well-oiled baking dish. Combine remaining ingredients and mix well. Pour sauce over fish. Bake in preheated 350°F oven for 20 to 25 minutes or until done. Serves 4.

CHAPTER TEN

Broiling

Broiling is cooking with intense, direct dry heat from a single source. Broiling fish must be done carefully and quickly. It is very easy to overcook using this method. Thicker pieces of fish, 1 inch or more, are preferable. Other methods of cooking should be used for thinner cuts of fish. Broil pan-dressed fish with the head for a juicier fish. Broil fillets, steaks, split fish, and chunks.

TO BROIL

1. Preheat broiler for 5 to 10 minutes (approximately 550°F).
2. Use a cookie sheet, shallow pan, or broiler pan and oil it well, or cover it with well-oiled aluminum foil. Turn up the edges of the foil to retain the fish juices and minimize clean-up.
3. Optional step: you can season the fish with salt, pepper, and paprika at this point, but it is best to season after fish is cooked.
4. Dust fish lightly with flour. Use a plastic or paper bag containing a small amount of flour. Put the fish into the bag, one piece at a time. Hold the open end closed with one hand and gently move the bag with the other hand to coat the fish. Remove the fish, and *gently* shake off any excess flour.
5. Set the fish on foil or pan, skin side down if skin has been left on.

6. Baste the top of the fish well with: butter or oil; half butter and half oil; half butter and half wine; or any sauce you wish to use (see recipes for baking in Chapter 9).

Fatty fish can be broiled without basting. Check the Fish Dictionary: mackerel, bluefish, usually dark-meat fish don't require basting. However, basting adds flavor.

Lean fish must be basted well and frequently during broiling. Lean fish will dry out faster than fatty fish.

7. Cooking time varies according to form:

Steaks: Broil 6 to 14 minutes, 2 inches from flame for the average cut steak which is 1 to 1½ inches thick. Place thicker steaks farther from the flame and cook 5 to 10 minutes longer. The average-cut steak does not have to be turned during cooking. However, thicker steaks do, and you should allow *more* cooking time *after* turning so the serving side will be golden brown.

Fillets: Broil 5 to 8 minutes, 2 inches

from flame. The heat source from broiler cooks both sides of the fillet so they won't have to be turned. If you have rolled the fillets, place them an inch or so farther away from the flame and allow more cooking time.

Whole fish: Smaller panfish should be placed 3 inches from fire. Cook one side for 5 minutes, turn, baste, then cook other side 5 to 8 minutes. Fluke, sole, and flounder do not need to be turned, but baste often during broiling. Larger fish are best baked or split and broiled.

Split fish: Place 2 to 3 inches from flame and allow approximately 5 to 10 minutes' cooking time. The cooking time can vary. Periodically, check fish for doneness. Do not turn, but baste frequently during cooking process.

Whitefish, carp, pike, and other fish with extremely delicate flesh should be placed 4 to 5 inches from flame.

If you use lemon juice or sauces during the cooking process, it is a good idea to move the rack 1 inch or more farther away from heat.

8. Check for doneness by inserting a fork into the thickest portion of the fish. The meat should flake without any effort. If it is not done, baste and return it to the flame for a few more minutes.

9. Season the fish after cooking and serve immediately.

FROZEN FISH STICKS OR FISH PORTIONS

Place frozen fish in a single layer on a cookie sheet. Broil about 4 inches from heat for 10 to 15 minutes or until fish is heated through and flakes easily when tested with a fork. Serve with tarter sauce or lemon wedges.

BASTINGS AND GARNISHES

- Herb butter or lemon butter (see Sauces and Butters, Chapter 17)
- For 2-pound fish: ¼ cup melted butter blended with 2 tablespoons chopped parsley, 2 tablespoons chopped chives, 1 teaspoon tarragon, ½ teaspoon thyme, 1 teaspoon salt, ⅛ teaspoon pepper, ⅛ teaspoon paprika, and the juice of one small garlic clove
- 2 tablespoons melted butter blended with 2 tablespoons vinegar, 2 tablespoons catsup, 1 tablespoon Worcestershire sauce
- A mild barbecue sauce (see Sauces and Butters, Chapter 17)
- Use a marinade (see Chapter 20) and baste with it after fish has been marinated
- Dust breaded fillets with seasoned bread crumbs and grated Parmesan cheese. Dot with butter. Broil 5 inches from flame until golden brown, without turning
- Broil 5 minutes for 2 pound-fish, remove fish and place drained fresh or canned fruit, such as pineapple, peach halves, orange or grapefruit sections, around fish. Return to broiler
- Or serve it plain.

BROILED FILLETS OR STEAKS

2 pounds fish fillets or steaks, fresh or frozen
2 tablespoons melted butter or oil
2 tablespoons lemon juice

1 teaspoon salt
½ teaspoon paprika
Dash pepper

Thaw fish if frozen. Cut into 4 portions. Place fish in a single layer, skin side down, on a well-greased baking pan. Combine remaining ingredients and mix well. Pour sauce over fish. Broil 4 inches from source of heat for 10 to 15 minutes or until fish flakes easily when tested with a fork. Baste once during broiling with sauce in pan. Serves 4.

BROILED PAN-DRESSED FISH

3 pounds pan-dressed fish, fresh or frozen
¼ cup melted butter or oil
¼ cup lemon juice

1½ teaspoon salt
¾ teaspoon paprika
Dash pepper

Thaw fish if frozen. Clean, wash, and dry fish. Place in a single layer on a well-greased baking pan. Combine remaining ingredients and mix well. Brush fish inside and out with sauce. Broil 4 inches from source of heat for 5 to 8 minutes. Turn carefully and baste with sauce. Broil 5 to 8 minutes longer or until fish flakes easily when tested with a fork. Serves 3.

CHAPTER ELEVEN

Charcoal Broiling

Charcoal broiling uses the dry heat from hot charcoals. The cooked fish should be golden brown outside and moist inside.

Whole or pan-dressed fish, or fillets, steaks, and fish sticks can be charcoal-broiled. Fish steaks with skin on them or whole fish with the skin intact handle more easily than skinned fish. Thicker cuts are more suitable because they will not dry out as easily as thinner pieces. Large fish are grilled best as steaks.

If you're using a whole fish, clean and scale it well. If it is thick-fleshed, make a few small slits in the flesh before cooking, cutting not too deeply. This is called scoring, and it hastens the cooking process.

Cut the head off a flat fish, like sole and flounder, in a diagonal. Also remove the tail with scissors. Remove any black skin.

Frozen fish must be thawed before charcoal broiling.

The proper utensil is a wire-frame grill, hinged, with two sides and a long handle. When you insert fish into the grill, the fish will be held securely in place and can be turned easily. This is important because fish flakes easily as the cooking process comes to completion.

If a proper grill is not accessible, wrap individual pieces of fish in aluminum foil. Put inside any herbs, seasoning, or sauces you desire. A small amount of butter, oil, or wine should be used. Close the foil securely and place on the grill, turning with tongs occasionally. Cook for 20 to 30 minutes.

For pan-dressed fish, sprinkle inside with salt and pepper and place 1 tablespoon butter inside each fish. Season outside with salt and pepper, dip in melted butter, then roll in flour. Wrap in foil and place in hot coals or on flame for 6 to 7 minutes on each side, depending on size of fish.

CHARCOAL BROILING WITH GRILL

1. Oil the grill well and heat it until very hot. If it is not hot enough, the fish will stick to it.

2. While grill is heating, baste the fish well with one of the following: fat; vegetable oil; melted butter; half oil and half butter; half butter and half wine; butter and oil with lemon juice; marinade. You can also place bacon strips around fish.

3. Place the fish securely in the hinged grill and the grill on the charcoal grill over the coals. The grilling of the fish must be done carefully. Small fish should be cooked quickly over stronger flames, whereas large and thick fish should be cooked slowly over

lower flames so the heat penetrates its thickness.

4. Turn and baste the fish every few minutes. Basting is easily done right through the frame of the grill.

5. Fish is done when it flakes easily with a fork inserted into the thickest section. On a whole fish, a fork should slip to the spine, without resistance.

Fillets: Take 5 minutes' cooking time, 4 inches from moderately hot coals.

Steaks and small fish: Need 10 to 20 minutes' cooking time, 6 inches from moderately hot coals.

Large steaks and fish take longer.

Whole fish, fillets, steaks need to cook 10 minutes per inch, measuring depth of the fish at the thickest part when laid on its side.

CHARCOAL-BROILED PAN-DRESSED FISH

1 3-pound pan-dressed fish, fresh or frozen	1½ teaspoons salt
4 tablespoons butter or oil	¾ teaspoon paprika
¼ cup lemon juice	Dash pepper

Thaw fish if frozen. Clean, wash, and dry fish with paper towels. Place fish in a well-greased, hinged, wire grill. Combine remaining ingredients and mix well. Brush fish with sauce. Cook 4 inches from coals for 5 to 8 minutes. Baste frequently. Turn. Cook 5 to 8 minutes more or until fish flakes easily when tested with a fork. Serves 2 to 3.

CHARCOAL-BROILED FILLETS OR STEAKS I

2 pounds fish fillets or steaks, fresh or frozen	1 can (8 ounces) tomato sauce
¼ cup onion, chopped	2 tablespoons lemon juice
2 tablespoons green pepper, chopped	1 tablespoon Worcestershire sauce
1 clove garlic, finely minced	1 tablespoon sugar
2 tablespoons melted butter or oil	2 tablespoons salt
	¼ teaspoon pepper

Thaw fish if frozen. Sauté onion, green pepper, and garlic in the oil until tender, approximately 7 minutes. Add remaining ingredients (except fish) and simmer for an additional 5 minutes stirring occasionally. Cool. Cut fish into 4 to 6 servings. Place fish in a shallow baking dish in a single layer. Pour sauce over fish and marinate in refrigerator for 30 minutes. To cook, remove fish, from marinade, keeping sauce for basting. Place fish in a well-greased, hinged, wire grill. Cook 4 inches from coals for 5 to 8 minutes. Baste frequently with sauce. Turn and cook for 5 to 8 minutes longer or until fish flakes easily when tested with a fork. Serves 4 to 6.

2 pounds fish fillets or steaks, fresh or
   frozen
2 medium onions, sliced thin
2 green peppers, sliced into strips
4 tablespoons melted butter

2 tablespoons lemon or lime juice
2 teaspoons salt
1 teaspoon paprika
⅛ teaspoon pepper

Thaw fish if frozen. Cut enough 12-inch squares of aluminum foil to wrap pieces of fish. Oil the foil lightly. Place one portion of fish on each piece of foil. If the pieces of fish have their skin, lay skin side down on the foil. Top fish with even amounts of onion and peppers. Combine remaining ingredients and pour over fish. Bring up foil and fold edges tightly, eliminating any air that may remain in the package. Place packages on a grill 5 inches from the coals. Cook 45 to 60 minutes or until fish flakes easily when tested with a fork. Turn the packages occasionally. Serves 4 to 6.

CHAPTER TWELVE

Frying

For frying fish or cooking fish in fat, vegetable oils and fats are preferable to animal fats. Vegetable oils can be heated to higher temperatures without smoking. Smoking is a sign that the fat is decomposing, and this will give the fish an unpleasant flavor.

The temperature of the fat is extremely important. If the fat is too hot, the fish will brown on the outside but remain uncooked inside. If it is not hot enough, the fish will absorb it, and acquire a greasy, fat-soaked taste. The best temperature is 350°F.

TO PREPARE FISH FOR FRYING

1. Thaw frozen fish.
2. Wipe the fish dry with a soft cloth or paper towel.

Whole or pan dressed fish with skin: Score pan fish over 1 pound; make slashes through the skin, but not too deeply. Scoring allows the thicker sections to cook properly in a shorter period of time. Moisten the fish with water, milk, one-half water and one-half milk, or beer. Coat the fish with flour or corn meal, or a mixture of the two. (It is possible to fry whole fish without flouring, but numerous breaks in the skin occur during cooking.)

Skinned fish (fillets and steaks): First dip fish into flour to seal in juices and hold fish together during cooking process. Then dip it into a mixture of 1 egg and 1 tablespoon milk or water that has been beaten gently so that no bubbles appear. Bread the fish by putting a handful of bread crumbs, cracker meal, corn-flake crumbs, or packaged bread crumbs in a plastic bag, adding the liquid-coated fish and shaking gently, supporting the bottom of the bag with one hand. Or, instead of breading, use a batter. Mix 2 eggs, 1½ teaspoons sugar, 4 tablespoons flour and add small amounts of milk until the mixture has the thickness of heavy cream. Dip dry pieces of fish into this batter and place them on a piece of waxed paper.

PAN FRYING—SAUTÉING

Pan frying is cooking fish in a frying pan with a small amount of fat. The result should always be crisp and golden fish with the center moist and flaky, but never greasy. Pan frying is the method most often used to fry fish; it is also the cooking method most widely abused. Thick fillets, steaks, and small, whole pan-dressed fish such as trout, sole, porgies, butterfish, dabs, sardines, and smelts are all suitable for frying. Thinner fillets are better when broiled, poached, or steamed.

TO PAN FRY

1. Use a regular frying pan for thin fish. Use an iron skillet for plumper fish. Do not use thin aluminum pans because they become hot too quickly and just as quickly lose their heat when the fish is fried. Electric frying pans should be set at 350°F. For stove cooking, use a medium flame. If the pan becomes too hot, the outside of the fish will scorch before the center of the fish is cooked.

2. Place a small amount of vegetable oil, or half butter and half oil into the pan so that it covers the bottom.

Heat the oil over a medium flame without allowing it to smoke. The natural fish odors will be absorbed by hot fats, not by smoking fats. To test the temperature of the oil, place a tiny piece of fish in it. If the piece of fish sizzles vigorously, the oil is ready for frying.

3. Do not put too many pieces of fish into the pan at one time, or the temperature of the fat will be lowered. Add herbs and seasoning at this point, if desired, or wait until after cooking.

4. Fry until one side is browned about 2 to 5 minutes. Turn and allow 2 to 3 minutes to brown on the other side. Fish should be turned only once. These times are approximate and vary from 2 to 10 minutes depending on thickness of the fish. Be careful not to overcook. (See Chapter 9 for another method for estimating cooking time.) Cook uncoated fish until the edges look crisp and brown and the center is yellowish to a golden brown.

5. Test the fish, inserting a fork into the thickest part. It should flake easily when done. A whole fish should flake to the bone.

6. Place fish on absorbent paper.

7. Season. Serve with lemon wedges or with a sauce. If seasoning was added during cooking, use the liquid with a bit of wine cooked in it as a sauce. Pour sauce over the fried fish just before serving.

Variations: After cooking add 2 tablespoons butter to the pan juices, 1 tablespoon fresh chopped parsley, and 1 teaspoon lemon or lime juice. When butter begins to brown (this happens quickly), remove pan from heat and pour over fish. Or, simply sprinkle with paprika.

FRIED FILLETS, STEAKS OR PAN-DRESSED FISH

2 pounds fish fillets or steaks or 1 3-
pound pan-dressed fish fresh or
frozen
¼ cup milk
1 egg, beaten

1 teaspoon salt
Dash pepper
1½ cups dry bread crumbs, dry cereal,
or cracker crumbs
Oil for frying

Thaw fish if frozen. Cut fish fillets or steaks into 4 to 6 portions and leave pan-dressed fish whole. Combine milk, egg, salt, and pepper. Dip fish into milk and roll in crumbs. Place fish in a single layer in hot fat in a 10-inch frying pan. Fry at 350°F or medium heat for 4 to 5 minutes or until brown. Turn carefully. Fry 4 to 5 minutes longer or until fish is brown and flakes easily when tested with a fork. Drain on absorbent paper. Serves 2 to 4.

SAUTÉED FISH OR SOFT-SHELLED CRABS MEUNIÈRE

4 fish fillets or soft-shelled crabs
  Flour
  Salt and pepper to taste
  Dash paprika
6 tablespoons clarified butter (see
    Chapter 17)

1 tablespoon lemon juice
1½ tablespoons chopped, fresh parsley
    or 3 tablespoons dried parsley

Put a small amount of flour seasoned with salt, pepper, and paprika into a plastic bag. Add the fillets or crabs, one at a time and shake the bag gently to thoroughly coat the fish. Shake off any excess flour. Heat 3 tablespoons of the clarified butter and sauté the pieces quickly until golden on both sides. Remove from pan and keep warm. Add remaining 3 tablespoons butter, lemon juice, and parsley to pan juices. Heat until butter begins to turn brown. Pour over cooked fish or crabs. Serves 4.

DEEP-FAT FRYING
This quick method of cooking is especially good for fillets and small fish like smelt. However, it is difficult to do correctly, and should probably not be done for the first time when guests are coming.

TO DEEP-FAT FRY
1. Have ready a deep-fat fryer, or a pan with straight sides, a fry basket to fit the pan, and a deep-fat frying thermometer. Or use an automatic, electric deep-fat fryer.

2. Always use vegetable oil. Animal fat cannot get hot enough without smoking. Always use clean oil but never use this oil to fry anything else because the fish flavor remains in the oil. Fill the fryer half full of oil. The more you use, the quicker it heats and the longer it holds the heat. Allow enough room for both fish and bubbling oil. There must be enough oil to submerge the fish completely.

3. Heat the oil to 375°F but do not allow it to smoke. Test the temperature with a cooking thermometer or drop a 1-inch cube of bread into the fat: the temperature is right when the bread browns in 1 minute.

4. Place the prepared fish into the fry basket, allowing enough room so that the pieces do not touch one another. This will prevent too rapid a temperature drop and assure even browning and complete cooking.

5. When the temperature of the oil reaches 375°F, slowly lower the basket into the oil to prevent too much bubbling. Increase the temperature slightly because when fish is first put into the oil, the temperature is momentarily lowered.

6. When the oil is the proper temperature, a hard crust forms almost immediately, holding in the juices and preventing any fat from soaking in.

7. The fish takes 3 to 5 minutes to cook. When it is done, it rises to the surface of the oil. Remove the pieces that rise to the surface and drain on absorbent paper. Season. (See Chapter 9 for another method for estimating cooking time.)

8. Do not fry any more pieces until the temperature has again reached 375°F. Keep the fish that is done in a low oven or on an electric heating dish. Serve with a sauce or lemon wedges.

DEEP-FAT FRIED FILLETS, STEAKS OR PAN-DRESSED FISH

2 pounds fish fillets or steaks, or 1 3-pound pan-dressed fish fresh or frozen
¼ cup milk
1 egg, beaten
1 teaspoon salt
Dash pepper
1½ cups dry, cubed bread, dry cereal, cracker crumbs, or bread crumbs
Oil for frying

Thaw fish if frozen. Cut fish fillets or steaks into 4 to 6 portions but leave pan-dressed fish whole. Combine milk, egg, salt, and pepper. Dip fish in milk mixture and roll in crumbs. Place in a single layer in a fry basket.

Fry in deep fat, 375°F for 3 to 5 minutes or until fish is brown and flakes easily when tested with a fork. Drain on absorbent paper. Serves 4 to 6.

OVEN FRYING

This is a hot-oven method. The result resembles fried fish.

TO OVEN FRY

1. Dip pieces of fish into seasoned milk, beer, beaten egg, wine, or french dressing. Coat with toasted dry, fine bread crumbs.
2. Oil a shallow baking pan. Place fish in the pan. Pour a mixture of half oil and half melted butter over the fish.
3. Bake in a preheated oven at 500°F. The fish doesn't have to be turned, basted, or too carefully watched.
4. Cooking time is usually 10 to 15 minutes. A brown crust will form, sealing in the juices. (See Chapter 9 for another method for estimating cooking time.)
5. Serve with a sauce or lemon wedges.

OVEN-FRIED FILLETS OR STEAKS

2 pounds fish fillets or steaks, fresh or frozen
½ cup milk
1 teaspoon salt
1½ cups bread crumbs or dry cereal
¼ cup clarified butter (see Chapter 17)

Thaw fish if frozen. Cut fish into 4 to 6 portions. Combine milk and salt. Dip fish in milk so crumbs will adhere well, and roll in crumbs. Place fish in a single layer, skin side down (if the skin is left on) on a well-greased baking pan. Pour butter over fish. Bake in a 500°F oven for 10 to 15 minutes or until fish is brown and flakes easily when tested with a fork. Serves 4 to 6.

CHAPTER THIRTEEN

Braising

Braising is suitable only for large whole fish or large chunks of fish.

TO BRAISE

1. In a frying pan, sauté 4 sliced carrots, 4 sliced, small onions, 3 stalks of celery thickly sliced, and 1 clove of minced garlic, in 3 tablespoons of butter for approximately 5 minutes. Put cooked vegetables in a baking dish large enough to hold the fish.

2. Lay the fish on top of these vegetables. (Fish can be wrapped in cheesecloth to prevent falling apart when removing it from dish). Add a bouquet garni (see Chapter 23) and salt and pepper. A few strips of bacon can be placed on top of the fish to prevent drying and add flavor. Cover and bake in a preheated 350°F oven for 20 minutes.

3. Remove baking dish from oven and place on top of the stove. Add a fumet (see Chapter 19) and enough liquid to cover the fish half way. The liquid can be white or red wine, or half wine and half fish stock. If you use red wine, enhance the fumet with an extra pinch of thyme.

4. Bring liquid to a boil, cover, and simmer until the fish flakes when a fork is inserted.

5. Remove fish from dish. (If cheesecloth was used, remove carefully to keep fish in one piece).

6. Reduce the liquid by boiling, and add a bit of arrowroot to thicken. Serve sauce with the fish.

7. Garnish with mushrooms, lemon slices, or anchovy fillets.

CHAPTER FOURTEEN

Steaming

With this method, the fish cooks in the steam that is produced from a boiling liquid. The liquid itself does not touch the fish. The natural juices of the fish are conserved and the fish does not dry out or shrivel. Either fresh or frozen fish may be steamed. If you steam fish often, use a steam cooker with a rack and a tight-fitting cover. But any deep pan with a contraption that prevents the fish from coming into contact with the liquid will do as well.

Any of the following liquids can be used:

- Plain water
- Water seasoned with herbs and spices
- Fish stock
- Water with vinegar
- Water flavored with wine

STEAMED FISH

1½ pounds fish fillets, steaks, or pan-dressed fish, fresh or frozen
1 quart half water, half white wine, boiling

Thaw fish if frozen. Place fish in a well-greased steamer pan. Cover and cook over boiling liquid for 5 to 10 minutes or until

TO STEAM

1. Dry with paper towel or soft cloth.
2. Cover the steaming rack with cheese-cloth, leaving enough on each side to be used as handles when removing the fish. During the cooking process, the sides of the cloth can be laid on top of the fish.
3. Bring the liquid to a boil.
4. Put the fish on the steaming rack and place the rack into the pan, without letting it touch the liquid. Cover.
5. Steaming time can be from 5 to 10 minutes. Fish less than 2-inches thick takes about 1 minute per ounce to cook. Test fish for doneness by inserting a fork into the thickest part of the fish. It should flake easily.
6. Remove fish.
7. Season after cooking. Prepare a sauce from the seasoned liquid or serve plain with lemon slices.

½ teaspoon tarragon, added to water-wine mixture
salt

fish flakes easily when tested with a fork. Cool. Remove skin and bones. Season. Makes 2 servings.

CHAPTER FIFTEEN

Poaching

Poaching is a method of cooking fish in a liquid by slow penetration of heat.

The following liquids can be used:

- Water, lightly salted
- Water, seasoned with herbs and spices, such as garlic, onion, cloves, parsley, celery
- Mixture of milk, white wine, and water
- Court bouillon, prepared in advance by boiling carrots, celery, onion, and spices in a fish stock, then straining. Only the liquid is used (see Bouillons, Chapter 19)
- Fish stock, prepared in advance (see Fish Stock, Chapter 18)

Whole fish, dressed (striped bass, sea bass, red snapper) are best poached in salted water. These fish are very flavorful themselves and don't need any seasoning.

Lean, white-meated fish (halibut, whiting, cod) are not usually poached, but can be done in a mixture of water, milk, and a dash of salt.

Large trout and salmon steaks can be poached in any of the above liquids.

Tuna, filleted or steaked, is excellent poached in any of the above liquids.

TO POACH

1. Wipe fish dry with paper towels or a soft cloth.
2. Wrap fish in cheesecloth to prevent it from falling apart, and make sure there is enough cloth at both ends to use as handles for lifting the fish in and out of the liquid. Wet the cheesecloth with the bouillon you are using.
3. Use a wide, shallow pan, large enough to hold the fish (a roasting pan is a good poacher). Put 1½ to 2 inches of liquid into the pan so that it barely covers the fish. Approximately 1¾ pint of liquid is required for ½ pound of fish; 6 quarts for 4 pounds of fish.
4. Add 2 tablespoons of vegetable oil or margarine to the liquid and bring it to a boil.
5. Gently put the fish into the pot. Cover and lower the flame, or place in 350°F oven and simmer.

Fish pieces	5 to 10 minutes
2-pound fish	10 minutes
4-pound fish	15 minutes
6-pound fish	20 minutes
8-to-10-pound fish	30 minutes

For small fish under 2 pounds, allow 5 to 8 minutes per pound. Or cook 10 minutes per inch of thickness (see Chapter 9 for estimating cook times).

6. Remove fish by grasping the cheese-cloth handles. Fish is delicate once cooked so proceed slowly and carefully.

7. Reduce the liquid by boiling, add a little arrowroot to thicken quickly, and season. Or, serve fish with another sauce, or with lemon wedges.

POACHED FILLETS MORNAY

Poach fillets of sole, cod, mackerel, ocean perch, or salmon in salted water. Arrange the poached fillets on a bed of cooked spinach lightly flavored with nutmeg. Top with Sauce Mornay (see Chapter 17). Sprinkle with grated Parmesan cheese. Broil for a few minutes until the cheese turns brown.

When using salmon, season the spinach with garlic, tarragon, and lemon juice. The cheese can be omitted.

BOILING FISH

Use the same procedure for poaching, except cover fish completely with the liquid.

CHAPTER SIXTEEN

Cooking Shellfish (Shrimp, lobster, crabs)

Shellfish must be cooked as soon as possible after they are caught. As soon as shellfish leave the water a dehydration process begins that quickly results in loss of flavor and spoilage.

TO SERVE WITHOUT A SAUCE

1. If the shellfish is shelled, simmer the shells and heads in 2 quarts of water for 30 minutes.

2. Then combine 1 quart of the liquid with: 1 quart red wine or 1 quart dry white wine; 1 bouquet garni (thyme, parsley, and leeks, for example); 2 stalks of celery, coarsely chopped; 1 sliced onion; 4 cloves; 3 carrots coarsely chopped; 1 tablespoon salt; and the shells. Cook for 20 minutes longer.

3. Add shellfish and cook for the times specified in the Fish Dictionary.

4. Or, if you are cooking the shellfish in the shell, follow step 2 and cook for 40 minutes. Then add whole shellfish and cook according to directions in the Fish Dictionary.

TO SERVE WITH A SAUCE

Simmer the shellfish in salted water, along with the shells, if available. Cook according to directions for the particular variety in the Fish Dictionary.

PART FOUR

Fish Cookery Basics and Accompaniments

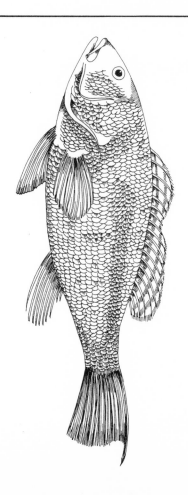

CHAPTER SEVENTEEN

Sauces and Butters

Most of the sauces and butters in this chapter involve heating butter either in a saucepan or, better yet, in the pan in which the fish was cooked. To prevent the sauce from burning before the seasonings and flavors have had a chance to blend, clarify the butter in the following way before using it. (A supply of clarified butter will keep for several weeks in the refrigerator.)

CLARIFIED BUTTER (Ghee)

Melt butter in a saucepan, a small piece at a time, pouring it off into a bowl as it melts to avoid burning. Allow the melted butter to stand in the bowl and skim the foam-like substance from the surface. A white sediment will settle at the bottom of the bowl. Carefully pour the clear butter from the bowl, leaving the sediment, or strain the liquid butter through cheesecloth.

ALMOND BUTTER for broiled or baked fish

½ cup almonds slivered
3 tablespoons butter
½ teaspoon salt or 2 drops Tabasco
    sauce

2 tablespoons lemon or lime juice

Sauté almonds in the butter until they turn a golden brown. Add remaining ingredients. Pour over cooked fish.

ANCHOVY BUTTER

1 teaspoon anchovy paste
3 tablespoons butter
1 tablespoon chopped, fresh parsley
    or ½ tablespoon parsley flakes

2 tablespoons lemon juice
½ teaspoon paprika

Combine all ingredients, mixing well, and add to pan in which fish was cooked. Pour over cooked fish just before serving.

ANCHOVY SAUCE

3 anchovy fillets, washed and
    pounded to a paste
2 tablespoons butter
2 tablespoons flour

1 cup milk
1 small onion stuck with 3 cloves
½ bay leaf

Melt butter in a saucepan. Add flour and stir for a few minutes over low heat. Add milk very gradually, stirring constantly to prevent lumps. Add onion, bay leaf, and anchovy. Simmer for 5 minutes. Remove onion and bay leaf and pour over cooked fish. Makes approximately 1 cup.

AVOCADO SAUCE for shellfish

1 avocado, peeled and pitted
2 teaspoons lemon or lime juice
1 teaspoon Worcestershire sauce

1 cup sour cream
    Pinch cayenne pepper

Force avocado through a sieve. Mix well all ingredients and serve, poured over cooked shellfish or on the side as a dip. Makes approximately 2 cups.

BARBECUE SAUCE for fish and shrimp

¼ pound butter, melted
1 clove garlic, finely chopped
½ cup catsup
¼ cup wine vinegar
2 tablespoons Worcestershire sauce
1 teaspoon chili powder
1 teaspoon salt

¼ teaspoon pepper
4 drops Tabasco sauce
¼ cup water
1 teaspoon arrowroot or cornstarch
    combined with a small amount of
    water to thin

Sauté garlic in butter until it turns golden brown. Add remaining ingredients to garlic mixture and bring to a boil. Add arrowroot and cook until sauce thickens. Use sauce to baste seafood.

SWEET BARBECUE SAUCE

(Best with Charcoal-broiled Fish.)

- 2 onions, minced
- ¼ cup oil
- ½ cup steak sauce
- 1 teaspoon dried basil
- ¼ teaspoon dried dill

- 1 cup tomato paste
- ¼ cup Worcestershire sauce
- 1 teaspoon dry mustard
- ½ cup honey
- 1 teaspoon salt
- ½ cup dry red wine

Sauté onions in oil until golden brown. Add remaining ingredients except wine. Simmer for ten minutes, stirring constantly. Add wine and bring sauce to the boiling point. Add more seasoning, if necessary. Makes approximately 2 cups.

Note: Onion can be strained through a sieve or left in sauce. Baste seafood with the sauce while cooking.

SHRIMP BARBECUE SAUCE

- ½ cup pineapple juice, unsweetened
- 2 teaspoons brown sugar

- 2 teaspoons lemon juice
- 1 teaspoon soy sauce

Combine all ingredients, mixing well. Use mixture to baste shrimp while cooking. Makes approximately ½ cup.

BÉARNAISE SAUCE

- 1 teaspoon dried tarragon
- ½ teaspoon dried chervil
- 1 large shallot, minced

- 1 tablespoon wine vinegar
- 2 tablespoons dry white wine

Combine all ingredients, mixing well. Cook over high heat until reduced to 1 tablespoon.

Add to 1 cup warm Hollandaise sauce (see recipe in this chapter).

BÉCHAMEL SAUCE

3 tablespoons butter
3 tablespoons flour
2 cups scalded milk, or 1 cup milk
    and 1 cup warm fish stock

Salt and white pepper to taste

Melt butter in a saucepan. Stir in flour and cook over very low heat for 2 minutes. Gradually add liquid, stirring constantly until sauce thickens. Season to taste with salt and pepper. Makes 2 cups.

Variations

- Add ⅛ teaspoon of mace and a pinch of nutmeg to the liquid.
- When using only milk, put 1 small onion stuck with 1 clove and 4 peppercorns in one cup of cold milk and simmer for 15 minutes. Discard onion and add second cup of milk. Continue to make the sauce.
- Add 3 tablespoons of tomato purée.
- Add 3 tablespoons of tomato purée and 1 to 1½ tablespoons of curry powder.
- Add 2 or more tablespoons of anchovy paste, 1 tablespoon of butter, and the juice of half a lemon.
- Add 1 cup of grated Cheddar or Gruyère cheese, a dash of cayenne, and ½ teaspoon of dry mustard.
- Add 3 hard-cooked eggs, thinly sliced or chopped.
- Add 1 teaspoon of chopped, fresh dill.

BLACK BUTTER (beurre noir)

6 tablespoons butter
    Lemon juice or wine vinegar to taste

In a saucepan, or the same pan the fish was cooked in for extra flavor, heat 6 tablespoons of butter until it turns brown. Add lemon juice or wine vinegar to taste. Blend well. Pour over cooked fish.

VARIATION
Add capers to taste.

BROWN SAUCE

1 quart fish stock (see Chapter 18)
⅓ cup sherry, dry or cooking
¼ cup tomato purée
5 mushrooms, chopped

4 tablespoons butter
4 tablespoons flour
    Salt and pepper to taste

Combine fish stock, sherry, tomato purée, and mushrooms. Cook until liquid is reduced to half (about 1 hour). In a saucepan melt the butter, add flour and cook for 2 minutes over low heat, or until mixture turns a golden color. Add liquid slowly, stirring constantly until the sauce is thick and smooth. Season with salt and pepper to taste and simmer for 15 minutes. Makes approximately 2½ cups.

CANNED SOUPS

Undiluted canned soups such as mushroom, chowders, onion, tomato, etc., make quick sauces. Add onion flakes or a dash of mace or thyme for a change in taste.

COCKTAIL SAUCE excellent for frozen fish sticks

½ cup chili sauce
3 tablespoons lemon juice

2 tablespoons lemon peel, grated
½ teaspoon prepared horseradish

Blend all ingredients well and chill before using.

BASIC CREAM SAUCE

2 tablespoons flour
2 tablespoons butter
1 cup milk

1 small bay leaf
1 small onion, stuck with 3 cloves
Salt and pepper to taste

Melt butter in a saucepan, add flour, and cook mixture over low heat for 2 minutes. Very slowly add milk, constantly stirring until sauce thickens. Add remaining ingredients and simmer for 10 minutes. Remove onion and bay leaf. Makes 1 cup.

VARIATION
Adding 2 tablespoons whipped cream will make the sauce brown evenly while broiling or baking, and coat the fish well.

HEAVY CREAM SAUCE for poached, broiled, or baked white-fleshed fish

½ cup mayonnaise
¼ cup heavy cream

¼ cup prepared horseradish

Blend all ingredients well. Serve with hot or cold fish. Makes 1 cup.

CUCUMBER SAUCE for cold fish

Peel, seed, and grate or finely chop cucumbers. Drain. Season with salt and pepper and white vinegar added to taste.

Note: 1 cucumber makes approximately ¼ cup.

CUCUMBER SAUCE for crab meat

1 large cucumber, peeled, seeded, and chopped
1 cup mayonnaise
½ teaspoon salt
2 tablespoons lemon or lime juice

1 teaspoon prepared mustard, French or English style
2 tablespoons scallion tops, minced
1 tablespoon sour cream

Blend all ingredients and serve cold over chilled crab meat. Makes approximately 2 cups.

CREAM CUCUMBER SAUCE for cold fish

1 cucumber, peeled, seeded, and chopped
¼ teaspoon salt
Dash pepper

½ cup sour cream
2 tablespoons vinegar (white, wine, or tarragon)

Combine drained cucumber, salt, pepper. Fold in sour cream and season with vinegar.

Add more salt and pepper and vinegar, if desired. Makes 1–1½ cups.

SOUR-CREAM CUCUMBER SAUCE

1 cucumber, peeled, seeded, and grated or chopped
1 cup sour cream
1 teaspoon fresh dill, chopped or ½ teaspoon dried dill

2 teaspoons chopped chives
½ teaspoon salt
½ teaspoon pepper

Blend all ingredients and chill for at least 1 hour before serving. Makes 1½–2 cups.

CURRY SAUCE

⅔ cup shredded coconut
1 cup milk
2 onions, minced
1 tart apple, cored, peeled, and
   minced
2 tomatoes, peeled, or seeded, and
   chopped
4 tablespoons clarified butter (see
   beginning of this chapter)

4 tablespoons flour
2 tablespoons curry powder
   Pinch cayenne pepper
1 cup dry white wine
   Cream (optional)
   Salt (optional)

Put coconut in milk to soak. Sauté onion and apple in butter until tender, approximately 5 minutes. Add tomatoes and sauté for 2 minutes more. Add flour and curry powder, blending well, and cook for an additional 2 minutes. Slowly add wine, then coconut and milk until the mixture is smooth and thick-ened. Add a pinch of cayenne. A small amount of cream can be added for a smoother sauce. Add salt, if necessary. Serve the sauce as is, or, if you want a smooth sauce, force the mixture through a sieve. Makes approximately 2 cups.

DILL SAUCE excellent over pan-fried, baked, steamed, or boiled fish

2 tablespoons butter
2 tablespoons flour
½ teaspoon chopped, fresh dill or ¼
   teaspoon dried dill

1 cup fish stock (see Chapter 18)
¼ teaspoon salt
⅛ teaspoon pepper

Melt butter in a saucepan. Add flour and cook over low heat for 2 minutes or until mixture starts to turn a golden color. Grad-ually add the stock, stirring constantly until sauce thickens. Add dill, salt and pepper, and simmer for 15 minutes. Makes 1 cup.

DILL BUTTER SAUCE

½ cup butter
1 teaspoon fresh dill, finely chopped
   or ½ teaspoon dried dill

½ tablespoon lemon juice

Combine all ingredients. Add mixture to pan in which fish was cooked or put in a saucepan. Heat and pour over fish. Makes ½ cup.

GARLIC BUTTER

½ cup butter
3 cloves of garlic put through a garlic
  press

2 tablespoons fresh parsley, minced,
  or 1 tablespoon dried parsley
  flakes

Blend all ingredients. Add mixture to pan in which fish was cooked, or put in a saucepan. Heat and pour over cooked fish. Makes ½ cup.

GRAPE SAUCE for broiled fish

1 cup white seedless grapes
¼ cup butter

½ cup dry white wine

Simmer all ingredients for 10 minutes. Pour over cooked fish. Makes 1½ cups.

GREEN GODDESS SEAFOOD SALAD DRESSING

½ cup mayonnaise
¼ cup sour cream
2 tablespoons onion, minced
2 tablespoons fresh parsley, chopped
1 tablespoon red or white vinegar

½ tablespoon lemon or lime juice
2 anchovy fillets, minced
  Crab, lobster, or shrimp meat,
  chunked or shredded

Blend all ingredients and chill well. Makes ¾ cup. Combine with shellfish until right consistency has been reached. Garnish salad with tomato, cucumber, carrots, watercress, or spinach.

GREEN PEPPER SAUCE enough for baking a 2-pound fish

½ cup green pepper, sliced in thin
  strips
½ cup onion, chopped
1 clove garlic, minced
2 tablespoons butter

½ cup water
½ teaspoon powdered ginger
⅓ tablespoon wine vinegar
1 tablespoon brown sugar
¼ teaspoon salt

Sauté garlic, onion, and green pepper in butter until tender, approximately 10 minutes. Add remaining ingredients and simmer for an additional 5 minutes. Pour sauce over fish before cooking. Bake (see Baking, Chapter 9).

GRILLING SAUCE

2 cups plain yogurt
⅓ cup freshly squeezed lemon juice
1½ teaspoons coriander seed crushed
1 teaspoon dried dill weed, or 2
    teaspoons chopped, fresh dill

½ teaspoon cardamom, crushed
½ teaspoon pepper

Combine all ingredients. Baste fish with
sauce. Serve sauce on the side with fish.

HERB BUTTER

½ cup butter
1 tablespoon parsley, finely chopped
    or ½ tablespoon dried parsley
    flakes
1 tablespoon chives, finely chopped

½ teaspoon dried tarragon
½ teaspoon dried chervil
    Pinch of dill
¼ teaspoon salt
    Dash pepper

Blend all ingredients well. After cooking fish,
blend mixture into the same pan and heat.
Pour over cooked fish.

HOLLANDAISE SAUCE

¼ cup butter, melted and kept warm
2 egg yolks

Juice of half a lemon, warmed

In the top of a double boiler, over boiling
water, mix egg yolks with a wire whisk until
they start to thicken. Add lemon juice and
blend well. Remove from heat and add
butter gradually beating constantly until
sauce thickens. Serve immediately over fish.
Makes ½ cup.

VARIATIONS
- Add 1½ teaspoons tomato paste to the
  Hollandaise sauce.
- Add 1 teaspoon capers.
- Add ¼ cup whipped cream into ½ cup
  Hollandaise sauce just before serving.
  This is known as Mousseline Sauce.

HORSERADISH SAUCE excellent for weakfish

½ cup sour cream
1 tablespoon prepared horseradish

1 tablespoon catsup
⅛ teaspoon salt

Blend all ingredients and chill. Makes approximately ½ cup.

LEMON OR LIME BUTTER

½ cup Clarified Butter
¼ cup lemon or lime juice
1 tablespoon fresh parsley, finely
chopped, or ½ tablespoon dried
parsley flakes

Blend all ingredients. After the fish is cooked, add butter to pan and heat, taking care that butter does not burn. Pour over cooked fish.

VARIATION
Add small amounts of prepared mustard to butter mixture until you achieve the desired taste. This is excellent with cod and haddock.

PIQUANT LEMON BUTTER

¼ cup Clarified Butter
1 tablespoon lemon rind grated
3 tablespoons lemon juice
1 tablespoon minced fresh parsley, or
½ tablespoon dried

Combine all ingredients. Add mixture to the pan in which the fish was cooked. Heat and pour over cooked fish.

MAYONNAISE

2 egg yolks
¼ teaspoon dry mustard
½ teaspoon salt
1 cup vegetable oil

With a wire whisk, beat together egg yolks, mustard, and salt. Add oil in a slow, thin stream, beating constantly until mixture thickens. Makes approximately 1½ cups.

VARIATIONS
Add vinegar (tarragon or wine) or lemon juice for additional flavor.

MAYONNAISE VERTE OR GREEN MAYONNAISE

1 cup mayonnaise (see above recipe)
1 tablespoon onion, minced
½ cup combination of fresh parsley, tarragon, watercress, and finely chopped spinach
½ teaspoon freshly squeezed lemon juice

Blend all ingredients and chill well before serving. Makes 1 cup.

MORNAY SAUCE for poached fish

2 cups béchamel sauce or velouté
    sauce (see recipes in this chapter)
½ cup grated Cheddar, Swiss, or
    Gruyère cheese

Pinch nutmeg or cayenne pepper
Salt and pepper to taste

Blend cheese in sauce. Add remaining ingredients. After fish is poached, spread sauce over fish and brown under broiler. Makes 2 cups.

COLD MUSTARD SAUCE for cold fish

1 tablespoon onion, grated
1 tablespoon prepared Dijon or
    English mustard
1½ teaspoons sugar

2 tablespoons vegetable oil
2 tablespoons vinegar (tarragon or
    wine)
2 cooked egg yolks, chopped

Blend all ingredients and serve over cold fish.

MUSTARD SAUCE excellent for mackerel

2 tablespoons butter
2 tablespoons flour
2 cups fish stock or bottled clam juice
½ teaspoon lemon juice

1 tablespoon onion, minced
1½ teaspoons dry mustard
1 teaspoon vinegar (tarragon or wine)
Salt and pepper to taste

Melt butter, add flour, and cook mixture over very low heat for approximately 2 minutes. Gradually add fish stock, stirring constantly until well blended and slightly thickened. Combine remaining ingredients and simmer for 10 minutes, stirring frequently. Makes approximately 2 cups.

VARIATION
Eliminate the dry mustard and vinegar. Substitute 1 teaspoon prepared English mustard and 3 tablespoons dry white wine.

OYSTER SAUCE

3 tablespoons butter
3 tablespoons flour
1 cup milk
1 cup of oysters and liquid

3 tablespoons fresh parsley, minced,
    or 1½ tablespoons dried parsley
    flakes
Salt and pepper to taste

Melt butter, add flour, and cook mixture over very low heat for 2 minutes. Gradually add milk and stir constantly until sauce is smooth and thickened. Add oysters, liquid, and parsley. Season with salt and pepper. Simmer for 5 minutes. Makes approximately 2 cups.

VARIATIONS
- Add 1 small onion stuck with 3 cloves, and remove before serving.
- Add 1 bay leaf and remove before serving.

PAPRIKA SAUCE

2 tablespoons butter
2 tablespoons flour
1 shallot, minced
1 clove garlic, minced
1 tablespoon paprika

1 cup fish stock or bottled clam juice
¼ cup dry white wine
1 tablespoon sour cream
Lemon juice to taste

Sauté shallot and garlic in butter until tender and stir in flour. Cook over low heat for 2 minutes. Add stock and wine gradually, stirring constantly until well blended and thickened, approximately 10 to 15 minutes.

Add sour cream. If you want a tart sauce, add lemon juice. This sauce can be used in baking fish or it can be added after fish is broiled, baked, or poached. Makes approximately 1 cup.

PARSLEY SAUCE excellent on sautéed or fried fish

2 tablespoons butter
2 tablespoons flour
1 cup milk, fish stock, or bottled clam juice
¼ cup fresh parsley, minced, or ⅛ cup dried parsley flakes

1 teaspoon lemon juice
Large pinch nutmeg
Salt and pepper to taste

Melt butter, add flour, and cook mixture over low heat for 2 minutes. Gradually add liquid and stir constantly until sauce is well blended and thickened. Add remaining ingredients and simmer for 5 minutes. Makes approximately 1 cup.

PINEAPPLE SAUCE

1 cup unsweetened pineapple, chopped

1 cup pineapple juice, unsweetened
2 tablespoons arrowroot or cornstarch

Heat pineapple and juice. Remove a small amount of juice and dissolve cornstarch in it. Gradually add to pineapple and cook mixture over very low heat until thickened, stirring constantly. Pour over cooked fish. Makes 2 cups.

REMOULADE SAUCE good for cold, cooked fish and shellfish

1 cup mayonnaise
2 tablespoons sour gherkins, chopped
1 tablespoon capers
1 tablespoon green onion, minced
½ teaspoon prepared Dijon or English mustard

½ teaspoon anchovy paste
½ teaspoon dried chervil
½ teaspoon lemon juice
⅛ teaspoon pepper

Blend all ingredients well. Chill in a covered container for at least 2 hours to allow sauce to ripen. Makes approximately 1½ cups.

RUSSIAN DRESSING for seafood salad

1 cup mayonnaise
1 tablespoon prepared horseradish
¼ cup chili sauce

1 teaspoon onion, grated
1 teaspoon Worcestershire sauce

Blend all ingredients and chill well in a covered container. Makes approximately 1½ cups.

VARIATIONS
- Add 2 tablespoons caviar.
- Add ⅛ cup celery, chopped.
- Add ⅛ cup sour pickles, chopped.

SEAFOOD DRESSING for seafood salad

¾ cup catsup
½ cup celery, finely chopped
2 tablespoons lemon juice

½ teaspoon Tabasco sauce
½ teaspoon salt
¼ teaspoon pepper

Blend all ingredients and chill well before serving. Makes approximately 1 cup.

SHERRY SAUCE for pan-fried fish

1 tablespoon flour
1 tablespoon water

¾ cup Dry Sherry
Juice of 1 lemon

Blend flour and water together until smooth. Add remaining ingredients and cook in pan in which fish was cooked. Stir constantly until sauce thickens. Pour over cooked fish or serve sauce on the side. Makes approximately 1 cup.

SHRIMP SAUCE

½ pound raw shrimp, chunked
2 tablespoons butter
2 tablespoons flour
1 cup milk, fish stock, or bottled clam juice

½ teaspoon salt
2 tablespoons fresh parsley, chopped, or 1 tablespoon dried parsley flakes
2 hard-cooked eggs, coarsely chopped

Sauté shrimp in butter for 4 minutes over low heat. Blend in flour and cook for an additional 2 minutes. Gradually add liquid, constantly stirring, until sauce thickens. Add the salt, gradually until you achieve the desired taste. Add egg and parsley. Pour over cooked fish. Makes approximately 1¼ cups.

SWEET AND SOUR SAUCE

1 15½-ounce can pineapple chunks, drained, save liquid
½ cup pineapple liquid (add water if not enough)
1½ tablespoons arrowroot or cornstarch

½ tablespoon soy sauce
¼ cup white vinegar
¼ cup sake (Japanese rice wine)
¼ cup celery, minced
¼ cup scallions, minced

Mix cornstarch and pineapple liquid until smooth. Add soy sauce, sake, and vinegar and cook over low heat until sauce thickens, stirring constantly. Add celery and scallions, and simmer for an additional 5 minutes. Add pineapple chunks and simmer for 5 minutes more. Pour over cooked fish. Makes approximately 3 cups.

TANGY SAUCE

2 teaspoons minced onion
2 tablespoons lemon juice
1 teaspoon dry mustard
1 teaspoon paprika

Dash cayenne pepper
1 teaspoon salt
¼ cup oil

Blend all ingredients and pour over cooked fish. Makes ¾ cup.

TARRAGON BUTTER

8 tablespoons butter
1 tablespoon fresh parsley, finely
chopped, or ½ tablespoon dried
parsley flakes

1 teaspoon tarragon

Blend all ingredients well and heat in pan
in which fish was cooked. Pour over cooked
fish.

THYME BUTTER

8 tablespoons butter
1 tablespoon fresh parsley, finely
chopped, or ½ tablespoon dried
parsley flakes
½ teaspoon dried basil

½ teaspoon thyme
¼ teaspoon salt
Dash pepper
1 tablespoon lemon juice

Blend all ingredients well and heat in pan
in which fish was cooked or in a saucepan.
Pour over cooked fish.

TARTAR SAUCE

½ cup mayonnaise
1 tablespoon olives, chopped
1 tablespoon onion, chopped

1 tablespoon fresh parsley, chopped
1 tablespoon sweet pickles, chopped

Blend all ingredients well and chill. Makes
¾ cup.

TOMATO SAUCE

1½ cups stewed tomatoes, fresh or
canned
½ cup mushrooms, chopped
1 tablespoon butter

1 tablespoon flour
1 cup fish stock or bottled clam juice

Simmer tomatoes and mushrooms for 10 minutes. Melt butter in a saucepan and add flour. Cook mixture over low heat for 2 minutes. Gradually add fish stock, stirring constantly until sauce thickens. Add sauce to simmering tomato-mushroom mixture and cook for 3 minutes more. Pour over cooked fish. Makes 3 cups.

VELOUTÉ SAUCE

2 tablespoons flour
2 tablespoons butter
2 cups fish stock or bottled clam juice

Melt butter, stir in flour, and cook over low heat until flour is slightly yellowish in color, about 2 minutes. Gradually add fish stock, stirring constantly until sauce thickens. Simmer for 10 minutes, then add remaining ingredients. Cook fish in sauce or pour sauce over cooked fish. Makes approximately 2¼ cups.

1 sprig fresh parsley, minced
½ teaspoon lemon juice
 Salt and pepper to taste

VARIATIONS
- Slowly add ⅓ cup of heavy cream to completed sauce.
- Add ⅛ teaspoon nutmeg.

VERTE SAUCE

Note: A blender or food processor is necessary for this sauce.

1½ cups fresh (see recipe in this chapter) or prepared mayonnaise
4 tablespoons fresh parsley, chopped, or 2 tablespoons dried parsley flakes

1 tablespoon dried tarragon or 2 tablespoons fresh tarragon, chopped
2 teaspoons dried dill or 4 teaspoons fresh dill, chopped
1 tablespoon chives, chopped
1 tablespoon spinach, chopped
1 tablespoon lemon juice

Blend all ingredients in blender or processor. Makes approximately 2 cups.

VINAIGRETTE DRESSING

1½ teaspoons prepared Dijon or English style mustard
 Salt and pepper to taste (approximately ¼ teaspoon each)

3 tablespoons vinegar (tarragon or wine)
9 tablespoons oil

With a whisk, blend mustard, salt, and pepper in vinegar. Gradually add oil, a few drops at a time, while mixing. Makes ¾ cup.

VARIATIONS
* Add 1 teaspoon chopped, fresh tarragon or ½ teaspoon dried tarragon, if you do not use tarragon vinegar.
* Add 2 tablespoons chopped, fresh parsley, dill, or chives.

WHITE SAUCE

---

2 tablespoons butter	⅛ teaspoon pepper
2 tablespoons flour	Pinch nutmeg
¼ teaspoon salt	1 cup milk

Note: Some cooks prefer to use a double boiler for making white sauce, but it is not necessary if you are very careful.

Melt butter, stir in flour, and cook mixture over low heat until flour is slightly yellowish in color, about 2 minutes. Add salt, pepper, and nutmeg. Gradually add milk, stirring constantly until sauce thickens, approximately 5 minutes. Simmer an additional 5 minutes.

This is a basic white sauce with many variations. Always serve very hot over cooked fish or cook the fish in the sauce.

VARIATIONS
* Add ½ cup minced celery.
* Add ½ cup grated, mild or sharp cheese.
* Add ½ to 1 teaspoon curry powder
* Add 1 finely chopped hard-cooked egg.
* Add 1 tablespoon drained capers and 1 teaspoon vinegar
* Omit nutmeg and add 1 tablespoon chives, dill, minced onion, parsley, pimiento, peppers, or mint. If using dried herbs use half the amount.
* Add 1 cup cooked, minced mushrooms
* Use fish stock or bottled clam juice instead of milk.
* Add a few raw mushroom slices.
* Add 2 tablespoons white wine or dry sherry.

WINE SAUCE (WHITE)

¼ cup dry white wine	1 bay leaf
¼ cup fish stock or bottled clam juice	1 clove
1 teaspoon scallions, chopped, or 2 shallots, chopped	3 peppercorns
	1 cup Basic Cream Sauce (see recipe in this chapter)

Blend all ingredients and cook over medium heat until sauce is reduced by half. Combine with cream sauce. Use this sauce for cooking fish or use over cooked fish.

WINE SAUCE (RED) excellent for dark-fleshed fish, carp, eel, etc.

1 cup dry red wine
1 tablespoon shallots, minced
Pinch sugar
Salt and pepper to taste

9 tablespoons butter, melted (clarified butter preferred)

Combine all ingredients except butter in a saucepan. Reduce liquid to about 2 teaspoons. Gradually add butter, constantly stirring, until sauce thickens. Pour over cooked fish. Makes approximately ½ cup.

CHAPTER EIGHTEEN

Fish Stock

BASIC FISH STOCK

1 celery stalk, chopped
1 onion, chopped
1½ pounds fish trimmings, bones, head, and tail of any white, non-oily fish such as sole or flounder, or haddock tails only
1 tablespoon freshly squeezed lemon juice

6 sprigs parsley
1 bay leaf
¼ teaspoon thyme
½ teaspoon salt
5 peppercorns
6 cups water
½ cup dry white wine
Pinch tarragon

Wash fish parts thoroughly in salted water. Put all ingredients into a deep saucepan, bring to a boil, reduce heat to a simmer, cover, and simmer for 30 minutes. Strain stock, discarding vegetables and fish trimmings. Stock is ready to use or it can be cooled and frozen. Makes about 6 cups.

EASY FISH STOCK

2 pounds fish trimmings, bones, head, and tail of any white, non-oily fish such as sole or flounder, or haddock tails only

2 quarts water
1 bay leaf
1 tablespoon salt

Wash fish parts thoroughly in salted water. Put all ingredients into a deep pot, bring to a boil, reduce heat to simmer, cover, and simmer for 30 minutes. Strain stock, discarding bay leaf and fish trimmings. Stock is ready to use. Makes 3 pints.

SPICY FISH STOCK

2 pounds fish trimmings, bones, head, and tail of any white, non-oily fish such as sole or flounder, or haddock tails only
2 cloves
½ teaspoon mace

3 stalks celery, chopped
6 sprigs fresh parsley
1 bay leaf
4 whole peppercorns
1 tablespoon salt
2 quarts water

Wash fish parts thoroughly in salted water. Put all ingredients into a deep saucepan, bring to a boil, reduce heat to simmer, cover, and simmer for 45 minutes. Strain, discarding vegetables and fish trimmings. Stock is ready to use. Makes 3 pints.

CHAPTER NINETEEN

Bouillons and Fumet

SIMPLE COURT BOUILLON

2 quarts water
2 sprigs fresh parsley
2 stalks celery, chopped
3 tablespoons lemon juice or red,
    white, or tarragon vinegar

1 medium onion, quartered
2 teaspoons salt
1 bay leaf
7 whole peppercorns
1 cup dry white wine

Combine ingredients in a deep saucepan and simmer 30 minutes. Strain. This recipe can be doubled or tripled, depending on the amount of liquid necessary for poaching or boiling. Makes approximately 2 quarts.

FANCY COURT BOUILLON for hot or cold fish

3 quarts water
1 quart dry white wine
1 cup red or white wine vinegar
3 onions, quartered
6 cloves
4 carrots, chopped

3 celery stalks, chopped
1 bay leaf
1 teaspoon thyme
5 sprigs fresh parsley, chopped, or 4
    teaspoons dried parsley flakes
1 tablespoon salt

Combine all ingredients in a deep saucepan. Simmer for 45 minutes. Strain. Makes approximately 4 quarts.

FUMET a very concentrated bouillon

2 cups water
2 cups sauterne or dry white wine
1½ pounds fish trimmings, bones, and

head of any white, non-oily fish such as sole, flounder, cod, or haddock

1 bay leaf
1 onion, quartered
1 carrot, chopped
2 stalks celery, chopped

2 tablespoons fresh parsley, chopped,
    or 1 tablespoon dried parsley
    flakes
Salt and pepper to taste

Wash the fish trimmings thoroughly in salted water. Put all ingredients in a deep saucepan, bring to a boil, cover, and simmer for 30 minutes, or until liquid is reduced to half. Strain liquid through fine sieve. Makes 1 pint.

BEER BOUILLON FOR SHELLFISH

½ cup minced onion
4 tablespoons clarified butter (see
    Chapter 17)
2 tablespoons flour

2 cups flat beer
1 tablespoon sugar
1 bay leaf

Sauté onion in butter until tender, approximately 5 minutes. Blend in flour and cook for 2 minutes. Gradually add beer until mixture is smooth and thickened. Add remaining ingredients. Cook until liquid reaches the boiling point. Makes 2 cups.

CHAPTER TWENTY

Marinades

MARINADE FOR SHRIMP

 2 tablespoons prepared mustard,
   French or English style
 3 cloves garlic, crushed
 3 tablespoons soy sauce
 3 tablespoons freshly squeezed lemon
   juice

 3 tablespoons freshly squeezed lime
   juice
 3 teaspoons oil

Blend together all ingredients except oil.
Add oil a few drops at a time, beating

constantly. Marinate shrimp 2 to 3 hours.
Marinates 1 pound of shrimp.

SHERRY MARINADE

 3 tablespoons dry sherry
 ⅓ cup soy sauce
 ⅓ cup oil

 4 cloves garlic, crushed
 ½ teaspoon chili powder
   Freshly ground pepper to taste

Blend together all ingredients. Marinate fish
for 3 hours.

CITRUS MARINADE

 1 cup freshly squeezed lime juice
 ½ cup orange juice
 ¼ cup freshly squeezed lemon juice

 1 onion, chopped
 3 tablespoons oil
   Salt and pepper to taste

Blend together all ingredients. Marinate fish
for 4 hours in refrigerator.

CHAPTER TWENTY-ONE

Stuffings

APPLE STUFFING

1 tablespoon oil or butter
1 small onion, minced
1 stalk celery, minced
¾ cup apple, minced
2 tablespoons fresh parsley, minced

⅛ teaspoon salt
Large pinch thyme
1 tablespoon lemon or lime juice
Paprika

Sauté onion and celery in butter until tender, but do not brown onion. Add apple, parsley, salt, thyme, and lemon juice. Blend together thoroughly.

Place fish or half the fillets in an oiled, shallow baking pan. Divide stuffing evenly on fillets and cover with remaining fillets, or place in cavity of whole fish and secure the opening with toothpicks.

Baste fish with a mixture of half oil, half butter. Sprinkle with paprika. Bake (see Baking, Chapter 9).

BREAD STUFFING

¼ cup celery, chopped
⅛ cup onion, minced
4 tablespoons butter
2 cups bread crumbs or packaged
   stuffing mix
1 egg, beaten

¼ teaspoon sage
¼ teaspoon salt
⅛ teaspoon rosemary
⅛ teaspoon thyme
Dash pepper
⅛ cup milk

Sauté celery and onion in butter until tender, approximately 5 minutes. Remove pan from heat, blend sage, salt, rosemary, thyme, and pepper, into celery-onion mixture.

Place bread crumbs into a mixing bowl; blend in celery-onion mixture. Gradually add milk, using only enough to moisten stuffing slightly.

VARIATIONS

- Add ¼ cup grated, mild cheese.
- Add ¼ cup minced, raw chestnuts.
- Omit milk; add ¼ cup minced, raw green pepper sautéed with onion.

- Add ¼ cup chopped mushrooms.
- Add ¼ cup nuts

CELERY STUFFING

½ cup celery, finely chopped
2 tablespoons butter
2 tablespoons parsley, chopped
2 cups fine bread crumbs

¼ teaspoon savory seasoning
¼ teaspoon celery seed
½ teaspoon salt
Dash pepper

In a saucepan sauté celery and parsley in butter for approximately 3 minutes. Add remaining ingredients and mix well.

CHEESE STUFFING

1 cup onion, minced
4 tablespoons melted butter
2 cups bread crumbs
1 cup grated cheese, Parmesan or Cheddar
2 tablespoons fresh parsley, chopped,

or 1 tablespoon dried parsley flakes
2 teaspoons powdered mustard
½ teaspoon salt
Dash pepper

Sauté onion in butter until tender, approximately 5 minutes. Add remaining ingredients and mix well.

CLAM STUFFING

12 littleneck or soft-shelled clams, chopped (save liquid). Discard necks on soft-shelled clams.
4 shallots, minced
4 tablespoons butter
½ cup mushrooms, chopped
1 egg, beaten

1 cup bread crumbs
2 tablespoons fresh parsley or 1 tablespoon dried, minced
1 teaspoon rosemary
Pinch thyme
Salt and pepper

Sauté shallots in butter until just tender. Add mushrooms and sauté a few more minutes. Add remaining ingredients except clam liquid. Add clam liquid if dressing seems too dry. Enough for a 4-pound fish.

FORCEMEAT (FISH) a very savory stuffing

1 pound fish (cod, flounder, haddock, pike, sole, or any white fish or combination)
Bread crumbs
½ cup milk
1 egg

4 egg yolks
Salt and pepper
Pinch thyme
Pinch tarragon
Heavy cream

Stir enough bread crumbs into milk to soak it up completely. Pound fish in a mortar or grind until thick and pasty. Mix fish with the milk-soaked bread crumbs. Blend in all ingredients except cream. Gradually add cream until mixture is smooth and thoroughly blended.

MINT OR WATERCRESS STUFFING

1½ tablespoons onion, minced
3 tablespoons celery, minced
3 tablespoons butter
¾ teaspoon salt
⅛ teaspoon pepper

½ cup fresh mint leaves, minced, or 1½ cups watercress, finely chopped
3 tablespoons melted butter
3 cups dry bread crumbs

Sauté onion and celery in butter until tender, approximately 5 minutes. Add salt, pepper, and mint or watercress. Continue to cook until all liquid has evaporated. Combine melted butter and bread crumbs and mix with all ingredients. Add water if a moister texture is desired.

MUSHROOM STUFFING

2 small onions, minced
¼ cup celery, minced
6 tablespoons butter
½ cup mushrooms, minced

¼ cup water
2 cups seasoned or unseasoned bread crumbs

Sauté onions and celery in butter until tender, approximately 5 minutes. Add mushrooms and cook for an additional 3 minutes. Add remaining ingredients and cook for a few more minutes. Moisten with more water if needed.

ORANGE-RICE STUFFING good for catfish or perch

1 cup celery with leaves, minced
¼ cup onion, minced
¼ cup oil
¾ cup water
¼ cup orange juice, fresh or frozen
2 tablespoons lemon juice

1 tablespoon grated orange rind
¾ teaspoon salt
1 cup cooked rice
½ cup slivered almonds, toasted in a
     skillet without oil

Sauté celery and onion in oil until tender, approximately 5 minutes. Add water, juices, orange rind, and salt; bring to a boil; blend in rice; cover; remove from heat and let stand for 5 minutes. Blend in almonds thoroughly.

OYSTER STUFFING

1 cup oysters, chopped (save liquid)
3 cups bread crumbs, bread cubes, or
     day-old bread torn into pieces
2 teaspoons salt
⅛ teaspoon pepper
⅛ teaspoon sage

⅛ teaspoon mace or thyme
3 tablespoons butter
1 onion, finely chopped
2 tablespoons fresh parsley, minced
½ cup celery, minced

Sauté oysters in a skillet about 5 minutes in their liquid, drain, saving liquid. Add bread crumbs, salt, pepper, sage, and mace. In another skillet, sauté onion, parsley, and celery in butter until tender, approximately 5 minutes. Add to oyster mixture. If mixture seems dry, moisten with more oyster liquid.

VARIATION
Add ¼ cup minced green pepper sautéed with onion.

SHELLFISH STUFFING

¼ pound lobster, crabmeat, or raw
     shrimp, chopped, or a
     combination

1 tablespoon lime or lemon juice
1 tablespoon light rum
½ tablespoon onion, grated

4 drops Tabasco sauce
¼ avocado, chopped
  Handful mushrooms, chopped

Combine seafood, lime or lemon juice, rum, onion, and Tabasco sauce. Allow ingredients to marinate for 3 hours in refrigerator. Drain,

½ cup bread crumbs
  Pinch each dry mustard, mace, basil
1 egg, beaten with 1 tablespoon oil

lightly. Add remaining ingredients except egg. Gradually add egg until mixture is moistened to consistency desired.

SOUR CREAM STUFFING

¾ cup celery, minced
1 onion, minced
4 tablespoons butter
½ cup sour cream

4 cups bread crumbs
2 tablespoons grated lemon rind
1 teaspoon paprika
1 teaspoon salt

Sauté celery and onion in butter until tender, approximately 5 minutes. Add remaining

ingredients and blend thoroughly. Makes 1 quart.

SPINACH STUFFING

2 cups spinach, cooked and well
    drained
1 tablespoon butter, melted
1 onion, minced

2 teaspoons lemon juice
  Pinch dill
  Pinch basil
1 egg, beaten

Blend all ingredients except egg, then blend mixture into beaten egg.

STUFFING especially good for carp, snapper, or sea bass

½ pound crab meat, cleaned and
    shredded (save liquid, if canned)
½ cup bread crumbs
¼ cup coconut, grated
1 clove garlic, minced
1 tablespoon oil
½ teaspoon salt
½ tablespoon curry powder

  Pinch each turmeric and powdered
    ginger
½ tablespoon cilantro, chopped
¼ cup bean sprouts
1 egg

Put bread crumbs into a bowl and moisten with liquid from crab meat, or water. Let stand 15 minutes. Squeeze as much moisture from bread crumbs as possible and crumble.

Sauté onion, coconut, and garlic in oil until onion has turned a golden brown. Add to bread crumbs. Add salt, spices, bean sprouts, and egg, mixing well.

CHAPTER TWENTY-TWO

Stews and Chowders

BOUILLABAISSE

1 large onion, thinly sliced
1 cup celery, chopped
1 clove garlic, minced
8 tablespoons oil or clarified butter (see Chapter 17)
1 pound white fish fillets (all bones removed)
¼ pound raw lobster meat or a combination of lobster and crab meat
¼ pound raw scallops

¼ pound raw shrimp, shelled and deveined
10 clams in their shells, cleaned Large pinch rosemary
1 bay leaf
2 cups fish stock or bottled clam juice
1 large ripe tomato, peeled, or 1 small can peeled tomatoes
¼ cup dry red wine Salt and cayenne pepper to taste Lemon slices

In a large saucepan, sauté onion, celery, and garlic in oil until tender, approximately 5 minutes. Add seafood except clams and sauté until seafood is cooked, approximately 5 minutes. Add remaining ingredients except lemon slices. Season with salt and cayenne pepper to taste. Cover and simmer for 15

minutes. Spoon seafood into large bowls, then pour liquid into each. Float a lemon slice on top.

VARIATION
Add ¾ teaspoon saffron during last 15 minutes of cooking.

MANHATTAN FISH CHOWDER

1 pound fish fillets or steaks, fresh or
　frozen
¼ cup bacon, chopped, or salt pork
½ cup onion, chopped
2 cups boiling water
1 can (16 ounces) tomatoes
1 cup potatoes, diced
½ cup carrots, diced

½ cup celery, chopped
¼ cup tomato paste or catsup
1 tablespoon Worcestershire sauce
1 teaspoon salt
¼ teaspoon pepper
¼ teaspoon thyme
　Chopped parsley

Thaw fish, if frozen, and remove any skin and bones. Cut fish into 1-inch pieces. In a saucepan, fry bacon until crisp. Add onion and cook until tender. Add water, tomatoes, potatoes, carrots, celery, tomato paste, and seasonings except parsley. Cover and simmer for 40 to 45 minutes or until vegetables are tender. Add fish pieces. Cover and simmer about 10 minutes longer or until fish flakes easily with a fork. Sprinkle with parsley. Serves 6.

NEW ENGLAND FISH CHOWDER

1 pound fish fillets or steaks, fresh or
　frozen
2 tablespoons bacon, chopped, or salt
　pork
½ cup onion, chopped
2½ cups potatoes, diced

1½ cups boiling water
1 teaspoon salt
　Dash pepper
2 cups milk
1 tablespoon butter
　Chopped parsley

Thaw fish, if frozen, and remove any skin and bones. Cut fish into 1-inch pieces. In a saucepan, fry bacon until crisp. Add onion and cook until tender. Add potatoes, water, seasonings (except parsley), and fish pieces. Cover and simmer for 15 to 20 minutes or until potatoes are tender. Add milk and butter and heat but do not boil. Sprinkle with parsley. Serves 6.

CHAPTER TWENTY-THREE

Bouquet Garni

BOUQUET GARNI for fish

    4 sprigs fresh parsley chopped
    1 bay leaf
   10 peppercorns, crushed

Pinch thyme
Pinch sage

Tie all ingredients together securely in a
piece of cheesecloth. Drop in poaching liquid
or in fish stews; remove before serving.

PART FIVE
Fish Dictionary

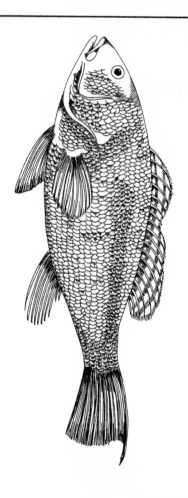

Abalone

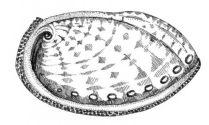

The abalone belongs to a large group of animals of mostly shelled and aquatic invertebrates called mollusks. The beautiful red or pink oval shell, sometimes called ear shell or sea ear, can grow to 6 or 7 inches long.

Because fresh abalone cannot be purchased in the United States outside of California, most people are familiar only with the lining of the shell which is the iridescent mother-of-pearl used for buttons and jewelry. The shell is permeated on one side with a row of holes through which the abalone respires and feeds itself. It also uses its radula, or tongue, to scrape the bottom of the ocean for food.

The large, edible muscular foot of the abalone fills nearly the entire spiral shell cavity. It has a unique, rich, and delicious taste.

LOCATION

Abalone is found around Catalina Island and Monterey off the coast of California in the Pacific Ocean. Protective legislation prohibits the shipping of abalone out of California because the supply is minimal.

MARKET

Abalone is available only in California. Occasionally, you can find canned abalone in gourmet stores in the East. Mexican abalone is available in cans, in chunks, or in flake form.

Buy ⅓ pound, fresh or canned, per person.

COOKING

Abalone is tough unless tenderized before cooking by pounding with a mallet. It will also be tough if overcooked. Thin, tenderized slices of abalone can be sautéed, baked, or broiled.

- (See Sautéing, Chapter 12) Slice thin and tenderize. Melt butter in a skillet and sauté abalone for 1 minute, turning once. Salt and pepper to taste.
- Dip slices of abalone in flour, dip in egg beaten with enough water to thin the egg, and roll in bread crumbs. Sauté in butter.

SAUTÉED ABALONE

1 pound abalone, prepared for
   cooking
3 tablespoons oil
1 clove garlic, minced

1 cup dry red wine
½ cup water
   Flour seasoned with salt and pepper

Coat abalone with flour by gently shaking abalone and flour together in a plastic bag. Sauté floured abalone in oil over high heat until brown on all sides, add remaining ingredients, cover, and simmer for 40 minutes. Slice abalone thinly across the grain for serving. Serves 2.

Barracuda

The barracuda belongs to the family *Sphyraenidae* that includes over 20 species. The barracuda is sometimes called the sea pike.

The barracuda's body is oblong and slender and covered with small, smooth-edged scales. Its long snout and mouth has large, treacherous, razor-sharp, fanglike teeth edged on its protruding lower jaw and palatine (membrane bones on the roof of the mouth). Usually the barracuda has a sharp canine tooth near the tip of the lower jaw. Its body is a beautiful silver that is darker on the dorsal side, with scattered inky spots, usually on the posterior of the body. The dorsal, anal, and ventral fins are black except for the margins. The pectoral fin is plain.

Barracudas average 12 to 15 pounds, but can weigh up to 150 pounds and reach a length of 5 feet or more. Most barracudas are savage and swift and have been known to strike bathers or anything that shines. The small, docile species are generally found in North American waters.

The meat of the barracuda is fatty with a strong flavor.

LOCATION
The barracuda likes tropical seas and is found mainly on the Pacific Coast. There is also a species in Florida, the Bahamas, and throughout the Caribbean.

MARKET

Barracudas are seldom marketed beyond the vicinity of their natural habitats. They are sold whole, steaked, and filleted.

Pacific barracudas are never poisonous, but those in Florida and the Bahamas have been known on rare occasions to be affected with the poison, ciquatera, which rarely kills but lasts a long time and is very painful. The poison infiltrates only the larger fish; smaller ones from inshore waters are nonpoisonous. There is no way to determine when caught whether barracudas are poisonous. It is safer not to eat barracudas from these regions.

The roe of some barracudas is poisonous and should never be eaten.

COOKING

Fillet and skin barracuda before cooking. The red meat, usually found around the stomach of the fish, does not destroy the taste but it can be removed easily, if desired.

- Bake.
- Broiled fillets: serve with mustard sauce or parsley butter.
- Sautéed fillets: serve with sour-cream sauce or mustard sauce with tarragon.

ROLLED BARRACUDA FILLETS

6 medium fillets
½ pound butter, melted (clarified butter preferred (see Chapter 17)
2 medium onions, minced
1–2 cups bread crumbs
4 egg yolks, beaten smoothly, without bubbles

2 tablespoons heavy cream
½ teaspoon nutmeg, grated
½ cup dry sherry
1 teaspoon salt
1 teaspoon pepper

In a skillet sauté onions in half the butter until tender, approximately 10 minutes; do not allow them to turn brown. Add enough bread crumbs to make a moist mixture and sauté for 2 minutes more. Turn off heat and add egg yolks slowly, stirring constantly until mixture is well combined. Add cream, nutmeg, half the sherry, salt and pepper, and mix well. Place equal parts of mixture on top of each fillet. Roll fillets around mixture and secure ends with toothpicks or poultry pins. Place fillets in an oiled baking dish. Combine remaining butter and sherry and pour over fillets. Sprinkle them lightly with salt and pepper. Bake at 400°F for 30 minutes. Baste frequently with pan liquid. Serves 4.

Bass

SEA BASS (Black Sea Bass, Groupers, Snook)
WHITE SEA BASS (Striped Bass, White Perch, Yellow Bass)
FRESHWATER BASS OR SUNFISH (Black Bass, Crappies)

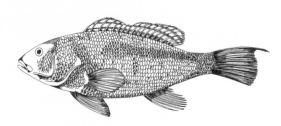

The term bass refers to fish of the family *Serranidae* (sea bass) and the family *Centrarchidae* (freshwater bass). Bass are found in both salt water and fresh water. Freshwater bass are called *sunfish.*

Bass are extremely plentiful (over 400 species) because they are so easily cultivated in ponds and can be successfully transplanted from salt water to fresh water. Striped bass is particularly adaptable. Bass are all flesh eaters.

Bass meat is white, firm, and—except for the white bass family—lean and mild-flavored. Smaller varieties are more tender than larger varieties. There are two inconveniences to dining on bass: the numerous bones and, in most species, inedible skin. The latter is not harmful but the taste is unpleasant compared to the delicious flavor of the meat. The following bass are the most popular and probably the most
familiar:

SEA BASS (black sea bass, groupers—including jewfish, and snook)
Sea bass are part of a large and diverse family including over 100 species. Their bodies are compact and oblong. Most species are blue with black stripes running the length of the body. The large mouths and sharp teeth are important to many of these fish since the majority are carnivorous.

The black sea bass weighs up to 6 pounds and grows to 18 inches in length. Its body is marbled with a diamond pattern of dark gray and white. Many females at maturity change their sex and function as males. The *grouper family*, from which the jewfish is the largest of the sea bass, reaches a length of 6 feet and weighs from 100 to 600 pounds. The grouper generally weighs less than 15 pounds when full grown. The grouper can change color and stripes like a chameleon, depending on the surroundings. They are extremely friendly and will take food from a human hand. The grouper has small scales, often embedded in the skin. Its mouth is large with big canine teeth in front.

The *snook* is mainly a southern fish and is rarely found in any other area. It ranges in size from 3 to 30 pounds and has excellent flavor.

WHITE SEA BASS (striped bass—white perch, yellow bass)
The *white bass* is shiny silver on the back, shading to gold below, with 6 to 8 darker stripes running lengthwise on the body. It averages 1 to 2 pounds.

The *striped bass* is blue or silvery, often brass-tinged, with paler sides on which 7 or 8 barely visible stripes run lengthwise on the body. It averages 1 to 20 pounds. Striped bass move into fresh water to spawn.

The *white perch* has an olive back with silvery sides. Small webs connect the dorsal fins. It averages ½ pound.

The *yellow bass* is brassy yellow with 7 distinct black lines running lengthwise on the body. It averages 1 to 2 pounds.

All white bass are strong-flavored, fatty fish.

FRESHWATER BASS: SUNFISH (black bass, crappies)

Sunfish include the black bass family and crappies. There are numerous species. Sunfish have round, flattened bodies, one dorsal fin with 10 spines, and no teeth. Sunfish are small, weighing only ¼ pound. Their color is brilliant but evanescent. There is a pygmy sunfish that grows no longer than 1½ inches.

All sunfish build nests on the firm bottoms of lakes that teem with fish and food supplies. The males of this species are aggressive fighters when guarding these nests.

Black Bass: large-mouth, small-mouth, and spotted bass. The black bass is the most praised freshwater fish in American waters. They are longer than the small sunfish and weigh from 2 to 3 pounds. Their size varies in different waters. Black bass are generally dull, golden green with a bronze lustre, often blotched with darker coloring. The young have black lateral lines which break up and grow fainter with age.

The *large-mouth bass* is olive or dark green to black on the back with silver sides and stomach. Dark lateral blotchy stripes extend from gills to tail. The upper jaw extends, past a point, behind the eye. The average weight is 5 to 6 pounds.

The *small-mouth bass* is greenish on the back and with a pale silver stomach. It has a shallow notch in the dorsal fin and the upper jaw extends to the rear of the eyes. The eyes are red in some waters.

The *spotted bass,* too, is a greenish color on the back with a silver underside. Below dark lateral bands that extend lengthwise across the body is a series of black dots. The body of the spotted bass is more slender than that of other black bass.

Crappies: This fish is the largest in the sunfish family, weighing from 1 to 4 pounds. There are only two species.

The *black crappie (calico bass, strawberry bass)* is silvery olive, mottled with clear olive green. Irregular, dark mottlings cover the body.

The *white crappie,* also called white perch, seldom weighs more than 1 pound. It has a compressed body with an indented forehead and flaring fins. It is distinguishable from other bass by 7 or 8 dorsal spines. Most white crappies are scarce in markets because of state regulations restricting their fishing season and sale.

The large 9-to-10 foot *ocean sunfish* is found only on the coast of California. Because of their habit of lying very still near the surface of the water, ocean sunfish have been called "floaters". Both flesh and skin have a tough, leathery texture, making ocean sunfish inedible.

LOCATION

All sea bass prefer warm waters and can be found throughout the world: Key West, the West Indies, off the coast of Texas, Florida, and California, and as far north as Cape Cod and the Pacific Ocean.

Freshwater bass are found in ponds, lakes, and rivers from New York to Vermont, in the Great Lakes and Mississippi Valley, from the Dakotas to Texas.

MARKET

Bass are available year round. *Groupers* of 5 to 15 pounds are marketed as steaks and fillets. Smaller groupers are sold whole. The scarce *jewfish* is sold as steaks, and if small ones are available, which is rare, they are sold as fillets. *Black sea bass* are marketed whole in ½ to 5 pound sizes. Small *snook* are sold whole and larger ones as thick fillets and steaks. *White bass* have a peak season from May to November. They are usually marketed whole in sizes of 1 to 4 pounds. Larger ones are filleted and can be purchased frozen. *Sunfish* are small and marketed whole in 1 pound sizes. *Black crappies* are abundantly cultivated in ponds and widely distributed, particularly in western markets.

COOKING

The skin of most bass, especially grouper and snook, has a soapy taste and is usually too tough to eat. If you cook bass with the skin, always taste the skin before serving, in case it should be removed.

- Large bass are best when broiled or very thinly sliced and pan fried. Bass is excellent in stews and chowders.
- *Grouper* is especially good when broiled.

- Small bass are excellent pan fried or baked whole.
- Charcoal or oven broiling works well with bass because it is succulent.
- Poach bass in salted water.

SEA BASS

- *Broiled or poached:* cucumber sauce with sour cream, Hollandaise sauce, serve with lemon butter, lobster sauce, oyster sauce, or tartar sauce.
- *Sautéed:* serve with tomato sauce, Provençal sauce. *Black sea bass,* when small, are the sweetest tasting prepared in this manner. Or marinate 2 larger fillets in lemon or lime juice for 1 hour. Dip in flour, again in juice, and roll in sesame seeds. Sauté until brown on both sides. Season with salt and pepper. Serve with lemon butter.
- *Cold sea bass* (See Flatfish and Salmon)

FRESHWATER BASS

- *Baked:* serve with any fish sauce.
- *Broiled:* broil one side, turn fillet over, spread with mayonnaise, and broil until done; serve with lemon or lime wedges and tartar sauce. Or broil without mayonnaise and serve with lemon butter.

SEA BASS

---

8 small fillets
1 teaspoon salt
½ teaspoon pepper

3 tablespoons butter
1 cup fresh, seedless grapes, peeled
Juice of 1 lemon

Season fillets with salt and pepper. Cook in 2 tablespoons butter until tender and delicately golden, approximately 5 to 10 minutes. Sauté grapes 2 to 3 minutes in remaining butter with lemon juice until hot and steaming. Pour over cooked fish. Serves 4.

BAKED BLACK BASS

3 pounds black bass, whole, with or
  without the head
1 teaspoon salt
¼ teaspoon pepper
½–1 cup bread crumbs or packaged
  stuffing

4 strips bacon
1–2 tomatoes, sliced
1 cup hot water
2 tablespoons grated cheese, Cheddar
  or Parmesan

Preheat oven at 350°F. Prepare fish for baking (see Baking, Chapter 9). Season fish inside and out with salt and pepper. Inside the fish arrange a layer of sliced tomatoes and place a spoonful of stuffing on top of each slice. Repeat the layering of tomatoes until fish cavity is filled. Save a few slices of the tomato for garnish. Sew or close fish opening with skewers. Place fish on an oiled baking dish and arrange bacon over fish. Pour hot water into dish. Bake for 30 minutes. Remove from oven. Lay rest of tomato slices on fish and sprinkle with cheese. Bake an additional 20 minutes or until fish flakes easily when tested with a fork. Serves 2 to 3.

Blowfish

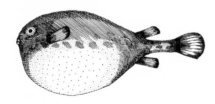

Blowfish acquired the name because of its ability to suck in air and water and blow up to the size of a large grapefruit when frightened. The blowfish is also called puffer, toadfish, globefish, as well as its most popular names, ocean or chicken squab. Its exceptionally juicy flavor is similar to that of chicken or frog's legs. Blowfish are meaty but their bodies are small. They are only 4 to 5 inches long and 2½ inches wide.

In certain varieties, the liver, intestines, and roe contain a virulent poison. In Japan, where blowfish is a great delicacy, only specially licensed chefs may serve it.

LOCATION
Blowfish are found in the Pacific and along the Atlantic Coast from Maine to Virginia.

Available from April to November, blowfish are sold whole and in a form that looks like chicken drumsticks without skin. When prepared in this form the blowfish is called sea squab, very expensive but delicious. Only the meat around the spine is eaten.

COOKING

If you want to prepare sea squab for cooking yourself, use the following method: hold the tail firmly with one hand and with a sharp knife remove the head by cutting through about 1 inch behind the eyes. Peel off the skin and remove the entrails. There should be one piece of meat with only the spine bone remaining.

Blowfish can be sautéed, broiled, or deep fried, and are especially delicious when pan fried to a crispy brown. To gain more taste, use a mild creamy sauce.

Bluefish

The bluefish is a marine fish and a member of the *Pomatomidae* family, a relative of the pompano and sea bass. Its beautiful, streamlined body is blue or green and there is an identifying black blotch at the base of the pectoral fin. Bluefish weigh from 3 to 12 pounds and can be as long as 30 inches. The flesh is rich and oily with a sweet, delicate flavor. Bluefish is considered excellent eating but does not keep well.

Bluefish wander spasmodically in dense schools. They are ravenous and destructive eaters; they will regurgitate in order to consume more food and leave behind slaughtered fish that were not eaten. A single bluefish eats twice its weight each day. Bluefish usually feed on menhaden and mullet.

LOCATION

Bluefish migrate from Massachusetts to Florida along the Atlantic Coast and are also found in the Gulf of Mexico. They like warm waters and are abundant in the Mediterranean Sea and Indian Ocean.

MARKET

They are generally sold whole in weights from 1 to 7 pounds and are available year-round. During the summer they are caught in Massachusetts and Maine; midwinter off Florida; March and April off the Carolinas; late April and May off Long Island, New York.

COOKING

Bluefish can be successfully prepared in any manner, but avoid using highly spiced sauces. Use anchovy butter, lemon butter, or parsley butter.

"Baby blues" or "snapper blues"—young or small bluefish—are plentiful in late summer. They are excellent broiled or sautéed.

Large fish can be butterfly-filleted, stuffed, and baked. Fillets can be cut and broiled. Scaling and skinning are unnecessary. Skinned fillets can be fried.

- Small bluefish are excellent pan fried. After frying, add 1 teaspoon tarragon to pan, deglaze the pan with ¼ cup of dry white wine, and pour over fish.

- Stuff a whole bluefish or butterfly fillets with a few sprigs of parsley, a pinch of fresh dill, and three slices of lemon. Dot the inside of the fish with butter and sprinkle with salt and pepper. Place the fish in a shallow baking pan on top of 5 green onions and 4 shallots, all finely chopped. Add 1 cup of white wine, dot the fish with butter, sprinkle with salt and pepper. Bake (see Baking, Chapter 9). Baste often during baking.

- Broil a whole fish split by the fish dealer, or use fillets. Place fish in an oiled broiling pan. Dot with butter and place a few bacon strips on top. Broil (see Broiling, Chapter 10) 4 inches from the flame until bacon is crisp and fish is cooked.

Butterfish

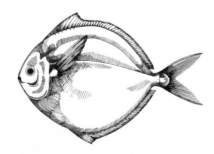

The butterfish is a member of the *Stromateidae* family and has a nearly perfect circular body with a tiny mouth. This small fish is sometimes referred to as the dollarfish, whiting, or pumpkin seed. It is silver. Probably the most tender of all saltwater fish, its meat is fatty with a soft texture that melts like butter in the mouth. Butterfish weigh only ¼ to 1 pound and are 6 to 8 inches in length, although there have been some that run to 10 inches.

Some species of butterfish habitually swim underneath jellyfish. They find safety and food there but are also occasionally killed by the poisonous tentacles of the jellyfish. Butterfish run in schools on sandy, bottom waters close to shore.

LOCATION

During the summer, butterfish are abundant in the shallow waters of New England, the Chesapeake Bay area, and South Carolina. They are found off Rhode Island during April and off Cape Cod in July.

MARKET

Butterfish are most abundant from April to December. However, winter fishing has developed on the northern shores of New Jersey, which makes butterfish available year round, especially in the East. The fish are sold whole, either fresh or frozen.

Smoked, drawn, and kippered butterfish are available in delicatessens and fish shops.

COOKING

- Butterfish is excellent panfish, sautéed or deep fried. Sauté with slices of oranges.
- Baked or broiled, butterfish turn a beautiful golden brown. When broiling, use plenty of butter and oil and place fish near the flame.
- Serve fried or broiled fillets of a large butterfish with a very mild sauce, such as Béarnaise.
- Smoked butterfish makes a good luncheon, served with lemon, capers or chopped onions.

Carp

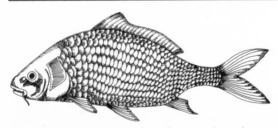

The carp is the largest and very abundant member of the minnow family *Cyprinidae,* which includes over 300 American species.

Among them are the bleaks, breams, chubs, daces, goldfish, mahseers, and squaw fish.

The colors of the bodies of carp range from dark green, brown, or red to yellow and silver. Carp have four barbels (whiskers)—two at each side of the small, suckerlike mouth. The mouth has thin, white lips that, in profile, meet at a wide angle.

Carp are rugged and tough fish with heavy, short, stout bodies and large thick scales, with the exception of mirror carp that have few scales and leather carp that have none. The back is strongly arched and the head small with a pointed snout. A complex bone structure in the inner ear gives the carp an excellent sense of hearing. Awareness of their surroundings is one of their outstanding characteristics. The carp is also noted for the teeth that line the throat area. It has a large spine at the front of the anal and long dorsal fins; each of these spines is serrated along its posterior edge.

Carp lay their eggs in the mud bottom and abandon them. In American waters, carp can weigh up to 60 pounds, and reach 3 feet or more in length. The average, however, is 5 to 10 pounds but are found larger in Europe. Carp can live as long as 60 years.

Carp feed mostly on plants, small insects, fish eggs, and crustaceans which they suck off the mud bottom. During this process of feeding, they stir up the mud and make the water impossible for other fish to inhabit. This activity sometimes gives carp a slightly muddy flavor, but the muddiness can be easily dealt with by cleaning the fish well and seasoning. The flesh of carp is lean with a sweet, delicious flavor.

LOCATION

Carp were transplanted into European and American waters from their native home in Asia. The Great Lakes, Mississippi River, and their tributaries are where carp are most abundant. The carp is referred to as the English sparrow of fishes because it has become so well established.

MARKET

Carp season is year round, but the peak is from October to March because they are more flavorful when caught in cold waters during the winter. They are usually marketed whole in weights from 2 to 7 pounds, but can also be purchased, on occasion, as steaks, fillets, chunks, smoked, kippered, or frozen.

COOKING

Carp is a very bony and scaly fish. If the skin is to be left on, scale the carp carefully. It is better to skin carp of any size. Large carp tend to be coarse and are best boiled or flaked, used in chowders, or ground and used in fish cakes. Small carp are best and can be prepared in most ways.

- Small, whole carp are good baked with pieces of anchovy placed in the stomach and gills. Baste with butter before and during the baking process. Serve with lemon butter, mustard butter, or almond butter. In Europe the head is served to the guest. In the United States the head is rarely served.
- Poach small carp in a water and vinegar bouillon. Serve with Béarnaise sauce, Hollandaise sauce, shrimp sauce, or white wine sauce.
- Cold, poached carp can be served with mayonnaise, remoulade sauce, or verte sauce.
- Smoked carp is available and excellent in salads and appetizers. It cannot live up to smoked sturgeon or whitefish, but has good texture and taste.

COLD POACHED CARP

4 pounds carp, steaked (see Steaking, Chapter 8).
½ cup parsley, chopped
2 tablespoons fresh chervil, chopped, or 1 tablespoon dried chervil
1 tablespoon garlic, chopped
1 teaspoon dried thyme
1 bay leaf, crushed
2 medium onions, finely chopped

3 tablespoons olive oil
1 tablespoon flour
1 cup water
2 cups dry white wine
1 teaspoon salt
1 teaspoon pepper
   Pimiento strips, capers, sliced olives for garnish
   Mayonnaise

Place carp steaks on a large dish and cover them with a mixture of parsley, chervil, garlic, thyme, bay leaf, and salt and pepper. Chill fish for several hours in the refrigerator.

Sauté the chopped onions gently in the oil until just golden, then add flour and blend thoroughly, letting the mixture cook for approximately 4 minutes. Add the water and wine, very slowly, stirring constantly over medium flame until well blended. When the liquid comes to a boil, reduce the heat, add the fish slices and cook uncovered for about 45 minutes over a very low flame. Remove fish to a serving dish and decorate with pimiento strips, capers, and sliced olives. Force the liquid in which fish cooked through a sieve, or pour it in an electric blender and spoon over fish when slightly cooled. Chill thoroughly, preferably overnight. Serve with well-seasoned mayonnaise. Serves 6.

Catfish

Catfish is a common name for the freshwater fish constituting the suborder *Nematognathi*. There are twenty-four species caught in the warm and cool waters of North America, a few of which are marine species. The catfish is related to the sucker and minnow and, like both of these, has an extremely sensitive hearing apparatus due to its complex bone structure.

Because catfish have poor vision, they depend on smell and taste to detect food. As scavengers they feed on both animal and vegetable matter and can survive as pets on grapes and chunks of liver. Some species have taste buds covering most of the body; food coming in contact with these is quickly devoured. The fish have long whiskerlike, sensory barbels that droop from large jaws. Their bodies are long and slender, the heads flat and shovel-shaped with little eyes. Their posterior fins are rayless, but the dorsal and shoulder fins have sharp, stiff, protective spines. Some species have poison glands at the base of the sharp pectoral spines that can cause a temporarily painful wound. Catfish have uniform dull blue or slate backs and pale or whitish stomachs, except for the madtoms and bullheads which are brightly patterned. They vary in size from the tiny madtoms (some less than 2 inches) to the largest and most important table fish, the blue catfish or Mississippi catfish, which can weigh up to 150 pounds. The small channel catfish is a very choice and popular food fish and weighs no more than 20 pounds. It has a beautifully slender body and a deeply forked tail. The popular bullheads with broom-shaped tails inhabit muddy ponds and streams. They reach 1 foot in length and weigh up to 2 pounds. The skin is scaleless, the meat is firm, oily, flaky, and very nutritious, with a delicate flavor.

Catfish farms have been established in the Mississippi River drainage areas of Arkansas, Missouri, Mississippi, Louisiana, and in other central and southern states. Fish from these farms are far superior in flavor to those caught in the wild.

LOCATION

Catfish are found everywhere in the world—in lakes, streams, bays, channels, and even in small ponds. They are found in the Mississippi Valley, the Great Lakes, the South, and the Middle Atlantic states. The marine species are found during the summer in bays and harbors of the Atlantic and Gulf states. The white catfish is located in the Pacific Ocean, the result of a successful effort to plant a species there.

MARKET

The season for catfish is year round, with peak months from April to September. Catfish are usually sold whole, but larger species are sold in fillets, steaks, and chunks. The average market weight is 1 to 20 pounds.

Farm-grown fish weigh from ¾ to 1¼ pounds. They hatch in the spring and are marketed the following fall. The blue catfish is considered the best eating of all.

Catfish are found inland, but they can be purchased frozen on the coasts. Marine catfish can be found if you live near the source of the catch. Canned catfish is higher in protein than canned salmon or tuna and the price is significantly lower. It can be found in gourmet stores.

COOKING

Catfish must be skinned before cooking because of the skin's leathery texture (see Skinning, Chapter 7). The meat is very oily, lending itself to many ways of cooking. The flavor of all catfishes varies according to the location and the water where they were caught.

- Small catfish and fillets are excellent broiled or pan fried.
- Deep-fat frying is the most popular method of preparation. Whole or pieces of catfish can be used. Serve with mustard sauce, remoulade sauce, or tartar sauce.
- Poach catfish in salt-water bouillon.

Serve with Béarnaise sauce, Hollandaise sauce, lemon butter, or lobster sauce.
- Cold catfish can be served with mayonnaise or remoulade sauce.

- Large catfish has a tendency to be coarse and strong-flavored. Cut chunks can be fried but they are best used in chowders, stews, or baked in sauces.

BROILED CATFISH

3 pounds catfish, cleaned and skinned	*2* teaspoons salt
¼ pound butter	¼ teaspoon pepper
12 sprigs parsley	*2* tablespoons flour
2 teaspoons fresh mint, chopped	

Preheat boiler. (See Broiling, Chapter 10). Melt butter in a saucepan. Brush fish lightly with some of the melted butter and sprinkle with chopped mint. Place fish on hot broiler pan, 2 inches below flame. Sauté parsley sprigs in butter over low flame for 4 minutes. Place broiled fish on preheated platter; add salt and pepper and garnish with hot parsley and butter.

Caviar and Roe

Caviar, naturally salty fish eggs, is taken from the roe of a female fish. The roe is the mass of eggs surrounded by a membrane that holds them together. The roe varies in size, depending on the size of the fish.

The roe is removed from the female before she spawns while the membrane is still hard. The membrane is removed to separate the eggs, which are then salted to extract water from them. The brine is drained and the eggs dried. The roe is then shipped fresh, frozen, canned, or jarred.

Different grades of caviar are determined by the size of the eggs, the degree of salting, and the resultant consistency. Large eggs with little salt are the best. The best Russian caviar is almost liquid and is difficult to preserve because of the low salt content. The most preferred caviar comes from the sturgeon and the sterlet in Iran and the

Soviet Union. This caviar is scarce because of past abuse of sturgeon fishing. It is now one of the most expensive foods in the world—over $40 a pound. Good quality caviar is gray.

Roe is also taken from other fish and sold at lower prices, but it is not cheap. Roe taken from the alewife, cod, herring, mackerel, mullet, shad; gray roe from the whitefish; red roe from salmon are available at reasonable prices. The shad roe, the most popular nowadays, measures 5 to 6 inches wide and 1 inch or more thick. Canned sizes are smaller but the flavor is as good as the fresh or frozen roe.

MARKET

Caviar is available year round, fresh, frozen, canned, jarred or salted dried. The fresh, canned, and jarred forms should be stored at temperatures below freezing (in the coldest part of the refrigerator, but not in the freezer), until ready to use. Serve chilled. The frozen caviar must be thawed in the refrigerator, never at room temperature.

SERVING

- Caviar is eaten mainly as an appetizer, served very cold in a glass bowl that is placed in a larger bowl filled with crushed ice. Serve with toast or dark bread on the side.
- Small pieces of lemon, chopped raw onion, sour cream, chopped, cooked whites of eggs, chopped, cooked yolks of eggs can be served as accompaniments.
- Use in omelettes with sour cream or cream cheese and watercress or spinach.
- Make thin, toasted sandwiches.

FRIED FISH ROE

6 soft fish roe	1 tablespoon lemon juice	
¼ cup flour	½ cup corn meal	
½ teaspoon salt	2 tablespoons butter	
¼ teaspoon pepper	2 tablespoons vegetable oil	
1 egg, beaten		

Wash roe and dry well with paper towels. Combine flour, salt, and pepper. Very gently, using two spoons or tongs, roll roe into flour mixture or put mixture and roe, one piece at a time, into a plastic bag and gently move roe around until coated with flour. Combine beaten egg with lemon juice and dip floured roe into it. Roll roe in corn meal or use plastic bag to coat roe with corn meal. Heat butter and oil in a skillet. Place breaded roe into fat and fry until brown on all sides (see Sautéing, Chapter 12). Turn carefully. Serve roe on hot, buttered toast. Serves 3.

Clam

The clam is a bivalve mollusk, its two shells or valves connected by an elastic ligament that allows the valves to open and close. The clam has a head inside the shell but is very primitive, without eyes or antennae.

Clams burrow into mud and sand by using their muscular foot that extends between the valves at the front end. Two siphons—one sucking in water containing oxygen and food particles, the other expelling water containing waste—are located in a single structure called the neck.

The sexes, in most species, are separate. Female and male deposit egg and sperm in the water. The developing larvae have no shell and are free-swimming, usually attaching themselves onto the gills of fish. It takes several months for them to reach an adult form. One species of freshwater clam has a brood pouch and the young are born with shells. There are hundreds of species of clams but only a few are sold commercially as food and these are extremely rich sources of proteins, minerals, and vitamins.

EAST COAST

There are two main species of East Coast clams: hard-shelled or littleneck clam and the soft-shelled or long-necked clam.

Hard-shelled clam: The hard-shelled clam is abundant south of Cape Cod, North Carolina, Florida, and all the way to Texas. In New England the hard-shelled clam is called a "quahog" or "quahaug." Indians made wampum from the purple portion of the shell. Today the shell is a source of mother-of-pearl.

"Clam" generally refers to the hard-shelled species except in New England where it means the soft-shelled variety. The smallest hard shell, under 2 inches, is referred to as a "littleneck" for its small siphon. Once the clam exceeds 2 inches, but not more than 3, it is called a cherrystone. The larger clam, more than 3 inches, is generally referred to as a chowder clam and used as such, chopped into smaller pieces.

The hard-shelled clam is very hardy. It lives in sand or mud, below the surface, but never burrowing too deeply for its short neck to gather food from the water. The clam is more likely to be found at low water than high, but can be found in water 40 feet deep.

Clams are commercially harvested by large mechanical dredges that look like houseboats. The digging instrument resembles a large iron rake with long teeth. Clams are scooped up onto the dredge and sorted.

Soft-shelled clam: The soft-shelled clam is found north of Cape Cod to the Arctic Ocean. Its shell is oval shaped and a little longer than the hard shell. The soft-shell burrows deeply into the mud or sand, stretching its long tubelike neck to siphon oxygen and food from the water. Small sizes are referred to as steamers and larger ones are called in-shells. They are dug out of the mud at low tide. The famous cockle is the European species. It has a convex, heart-shaped shell with ribs fanning out from a common center.

PACIFIC COAST

On the Pacific Coast there are approximately 30 varieties of clams. The most popular is the razor clam with its long tubular siphon, a tide-flat dweller that digs deeply into the sand or mud and is taken by digging at low tide. The famous Pismo clam is very succulent and is protected by law from over-digging. Other Pacific species are the butter clam, the littleneck (a different species from that of the Atlantic), the mud clam, and the gigantic geoduck (also known as gaeduck or giveduc)—an excellent eating clam but not obtainable in the markets. The giant clam of the South Pacific weighs up to 500 pounds and reaches a length of 5 feet.

MARKET

The peak of the season is October to April but because of forced breeding, clams are available in some form year round. They are marketed alive in shells, shucked, canned, or frozen.

Clams live in the shell: Clams in this form are usually sold by the dozen or pound.

Hard-shelled clams: Clams must be bought alive. If any of the valves are partially opened and do not close when handled, the clam is dead and must be discarded.

Soft-shelled clams: When the clam is touched, there will be a slight constriction of the neck, indicating it is alive and usable. Otherwise, it must be discarded.

Clams kept at a maximum temperature of 40°F will stay alive for several days. Soft-shelled clams are more perishable than the others: they lose freshness easier and are harder to handle.

Shucked clams: Clams removed from their shells are usually sold fresh or frozen in pints and quarts of waxed or metal containers. When buying shucked clams, check closely for plumpness. Their liquid should be clear and free from pieces of broken shell. They must always be refrigerated or placed on ice to keep fresh. They will stay fresh for a week, if stored properly.

Canned clams: Clams are available whole, minced, or in chowders. Clam juice and broth are available canned and bottled. The can sizes range from 3½ ounces to 4 pounds. Hard-shelled, soft-shelled, razor, surf, and Pismo clams are available in canned form.

Frozen Clams: Frozen clams must be defrosted in the refrigerator, never at room temperature, and once thawed must be used immediately and never refrozen.

COOKING

Clams on the half shell must be served very cold. Serve on shaved ice, being careful not to lose any delicious clam juice. Serve raw clams with condiments: pieces of lemon or lime, cocktail sauce, horseradish, or freshly ground pepper.

Shucking hard- and soft-shelled clams: Clams must be thoroughly washed with a brush. Make sure there are no broken shells or dead clams (these must be discarded). Hold the clam in one hand, the hinge of the shell against the palm. Insert a clam knife between halves of the shell and cut around the clam with a twisting motion in order to loosen the shell and open it. Soft-shelled clams are opened the same way; they are easier. Remove only one half of the shell if you are serving them raw. Detach the clam meat from the remaining shell by sliding a knife under it. Purchase 6 clams per person; more if the clams are very small.

If the meat is to be used for other purposes, remove it from the shell and rinse well under running cold water. You will need ½ pint of shucked clams per person.

If you dig the clams yourself, cover them with clean sea water or ⅓ cup salt to 1 gallon tap water and let clams stand for 20 minutes before opening them. The clams will discharge any sand inside, which settles to the bottom. Do this soaking with clean, salted water 2 or 3 more times. Finally, wash clams thoroughly and open the shells.

Steaming clams: Twenty or more steamed clams per person is the average portion, using the hard- or soft-shelled varieties.

- Thoroughly scrub clams with a brush and put them in a large kettle. Fill the kettle with ½ inch of liquid, such as slightly salted water, water with the juice of 1 lemon, half water and half white wine, all white wine. Cover the pot tightly and cook over a medium-high flame, steaming clams for 6 minutes or until shells begin to open.
- Before cooking the soft-shelled variety, remove the beard. With a stiff brush, scrub the clams clean under running water, pulling off the beards. The black part of the neck can also be removed, if desired. Any clams that do not open should be discarded. Strain the broth through cheesecloth and serve it in cups with the clams and bowls of melted butter.
- Clams in the shell are good baked, boiled, steamed, broiled, and for making broth and in bouillabaisse.
- Shucked clams are good baked, broiled, deep-fat fried, pan fried, in chowders, soups, stews, fritters, patties, pies, or served raw or as a cocktail.

CLAM CROWNS good as either appetizer or entrée

1 can (4 ounces) clams, drained and chopped	⅓ cup bread crumbs
2 tablespoons onion, grated	20 mushroom caps, large enough to be stuffed
1 tablespoon lemon juice	2 tablespoons butter, melted
½ teaspoon oregano	

Blend all ingredients except for mushroom caps and melted butter. Stuff mushroom caps with mixture. Drizzle melted butter over mushroom tops and broil until tops of the stuffed mushrooms sizzle. Serves 4.

MANHATTAN CLAM CHOWDER

1 quart clams, shucked and chopped (drain and save liquid)
¼ pound salt pork, finely chopped, or 4 slices bacon
1 large onion, chopped
1 green pepper, chopped
½ cup unseasoned bread crumbs
2 teaspoons salt
3 cups canned tomatoes or stewed fresh

2 cups water
2 carrots, chopped
2 medium potatoes, peeled and diced
3 stalks celery, chopped
¼ teaspoon pepper
½ teaspoon sugar
1 cup clam juice
¼ teaspoon thyme leaves, crushed

Sauté the pork until golden brown, approximately 15 minutes. Add onion and sauté until brown, about 5 minutes. Add all vegetables, water, and seasonings. Cover and simmer for 1 hour. Add clams and clam juice and cook for an additional 5 minutes. Add bread crumbs and stir well. Serve hot with crackers on the side. Makes approximately 2 quarts.

NEW ENGLAND CLAM CHOWDER

1½ cups clams, shucked (drain and save liquid)
4 slices bacon, cut into small pieces, or ¼ cup salt pork
1 medium onion, minced
2 medium potatoes, peeled and diced
2 cups light cream or milk (for a thinner soup)

Salt and pepper to taste
Pinch thyme
Pinch paprika
1 bay leaf
1 clove
1 tablespoon butter

Fry bacon or salt pork until crisp. Remove from pan and set aside. Sauté the onion in bacon fat until lightly browned. Boil potatoes in enough water to cover until tender. Remove potatoes and add bacon or pork, onion, potatoes, clam juice, bay leaf, and clove to potato liquid. Bring to a boil and simmer for 5 minutes. Remove bay leaf and clove. Season with salt and pepper to taste. Gradually add cream and butter. When liquid returns to the boiling point, add clams. Allow them to heat thoroughly. Sprinkle with a pinch of thyme. Serve in cups with a pinch of paprika and crackers on the side. Makes approximately 1½ quarts.

Cod

BURBOT   **LING**
HADDOCK   **POLLACK**
HAKE   **SCROD**

Cod are members of a very large family *Gadidae*. Their abundance makes them extremely important as food fish. The fish of this family are all bottom feeders, relentlessly consuming mollusks, crustaceans, starfish, worms, squid, and practically any other fish that comes within their range of attack. They have large, soft ventral fins, unusually situated either under or in front of the pectorals.

COD

There are many varieties of cod with as many variations in coloring. The most common is gray-green and reddish brown with whitish lateral lines. The back and sides have many round brown spots. The three dorsal fins and two anal fins are a dark color. Under the chin is a small barbel.

Most cod weigh from 2½ to 25 pounds, but cod weighing 50 to 200 pounds have been caught. They spawn in southern waters where they migrate from the North Atlantic and the North Pacific. A good-sized female can lay up to five million eggs of which only few survive. Still, over a billion pounds of cod are caught annually.

HADDOCK

Black lateral lines with dark side patches below them and above the pectoral fins identify the haddock. The body is dark gray on the back, with a whitish belly. The haddock has a small mouth. The flesh is white, firm, lean and has an excellent mild flavor. The average market weight is 1½ to 6 pounds, but 30 pounders with a length of 3 feet have been caught. Over 50,000 tons of haddock are caught annually.

BURBOT

Burbot is also known as freshwater cod or freshwater cusk. The body is an olive green with black lines or marbled crisscrossing on the back and sides. The underside is a darkish yellow. The fish is long and slender with a single barbel (whisker) dangling from its chin. It has very long dorsal and anal fins, a flat head, and pointed, fine, sharp teeth. The scales are very tiny. The average weight is 3 pounds. The flesh is white, lean, and flaky, with an unusual flavor.

HAKE

Hake is included here with cod because of their close relationship. Hake is a slender, long fish with a fat belly and an especially slippery skin. The average weight is 2 to 5 pounds. The hake has two dorsal fins, one of which is much longer than the other. Hake has a weak tail and one feeler and also extremely large eyes. The flesh is lean, white, and practically boneless, with a coarse and watery texture and a mild flavor. This soft-fleshed fish does not keep as well as other fish.

LING

Ling is also closely related to cod. The skin is thick and the body is long and slender and speckled with gray, brown, or yellow and brown spots. The darker lings are a beautiful green color. They can grow to 4 feet in length and weigh up to 40 pounds. Most, however, weigh about 4 pounds. The flesh is white and extremely lean, tending toward dryness. It has an unusual flavor if prepared carefully.

POLLACK

The pollack is a fat fish with a beautiful elongated body covered with minute scales. It is olive green with pale lateral lines—very much like cod, but darker and shinier—with a forked tail and a jutting lower jaw with no barbels. The average weight is 3 to 12 pounds. The flesh is white, containing more fat than other cod, firm textured, and well flavored. On restaurant menus, the pollack is often referred to as deep-sea fillets or Boston bluefish.

SCROD

Scrod is a young cod weighing no more than about 2½ pounds. However, most other young fish of this family are also called scrod.

LOCATION

All fish of this family are found in cold waters of the North Atlantic and North Pacific. Freshwater burbot are found in the deep waters of the Great Lakes, Northern rivers, and streams all the way north to the Arctic Circle. Similar burbot can be found in Asia and Europe. Hake prefer warmer waters

and are found in the Pacific Ocean from California to Alaska.

MARKET

Cod is available year round throughout the United States as steaks, center cuts, fillets, and flakes, or shredded, pickled, green or smoked, or in salted slabs. Usually it is in a frozen form. Canned and salt-dried flakes, shreds or fillets are also available. The average market size of fresh cod is 10 pounds. Smaller ones are available only if you live near the source of the supply, where they can be purchased from the fishermen.

Burbot is available from April to October and is usually purchased whole. A valuable source of Vitamin A is burbot liver oil.

Haddock is available year round in the United States. Fresh whole haddock weighing up to 3 pounds are also available salted and flaked, but haddock is sold mostly as fillets, either fresh, or, more frequently, frozen. Finnan haddie— smoked haddock fillets or whole fish—has a savory flavor. Over 100,000 pounds of haddock is consumed in the United States annually.

Hake is available year round and usually sold whole. Hake fillets are usually called haddock, cod, or deep-sea fillets. Most of what is sold as salted codfish is actually salted hake.

Ling is available year round, whole, filleted, steaked, chunked, and smoked.

Pollack is available year round and can be purchased fresh, frozen, smoked, or salted, in whole, steaked, or filleted forms.

Frozen fillets are particularly popular because of its firm-textured flesh. Pollack adapts well to freezing. Frozen pollack are labeled ocean-fresh fillets, deep-sea fillets, or other similar names.

Scrod is prepared as fillets or in strips, both fresh and frozen. Frozen scrod is very popular and attractively packaged.

COOKING

Good as plain or butterfly fillets and steaks, skinned or unskinned. Fillets can be fried, broiled, or flaked and used for fish cakes or chowders. They are good steamed, served with a mild or tangy sauce. Keep sauces delicate, and, when sautéing, use only herbs for flavoring.

- Cod is usually poached in salt-water bouillon, but a well-seasoned and flavored court bouillon can be used. Serve with lemon butter, Hollandaise sauce, or a bechamel sauce with a chopped hard-boiled egg and a bit of sherry added.
- Cod is delicious cooked with onions.
- Hake is excellent baked whole.
- Ling must be skinned. Small pieces can be fried; large pieces can be broiled or baked. The flesh is very lean and dries out unless basted frequently during cooking with sauce or butter.

CODFISH STEAKS

---

4 cod steaks	2 tablespoons fresh parsley, chopped
Salt and pepper to taste	Lemon slices and lemon wedges
1½ cups dry white wine	
6 tablespoons butter (clarified preferred, see Chapter 17)	

Arrange cod steaks in an oiled baking dish (see Baking, Chapter 9), season with salt and pepper, cover with white wine. Allow fish to marinate in refrigerator for a few hours. Before baking, place cod on lemon slices, dot cod with butter and bake, basting frequently with baking liquid until fish is done. Serve sprinkled with parsley and garnished with lemon wedges. Serves 4.

COD STEAKS ORANGED

---

4 cod steaks	3 tablespoons soy sauce
½ cup orange juice, frozen defrosted, and undiluted	1 clove garlic, crushed
¼ cup sherry	1 tablespoon oil
	2 tablespoons bread crumbs

Marinate cod, covered, in mixture of orange juice, sherry, soy sauce, garlic and oil for 2 hours in refrigerator. When ready to bake, put cod steaks on an oiled baking dish (see Baking, Chapter 9), and sprinkle bread crumbs over fish. Bake at 350°F for approximately 20 minutes. Serves 4.

SALT COD

2 salted cod fillets
Pepper
3 eggs, beaten
½ cup bread crumbs
2 tablespoons oil

2 tablespoons butter
Juice of 1 lemon
⅓ tomato sauce recipe (see Chapter 17)

Cut up salt cod into bite-size pieces. Season pieces with pepper. Dip pieces into beaten egg, then into bread crumbs. Fry them (see Frying, Chapter 12) in a mixture of half oil and half butter. Arrange cod on a dish and sprinkle with lemon juice. Serve with a tomato sauce. Serves 2.

SMOKED HADDOCK CASSEROLE

1 medium smoked haddock, skinned, boned, and flaked
2 cups cooked rice
2 hard-boiled eggs, finely chopped
3 gherkins, finely chopped

3 tablespoons butter
2 tablespoons fresh parsley, chopped
Salt and pepper to taste
Heavy cream

Sauté rice, haddock, eggs, and gherkins in butter until heated thoroughly, mixing carefully to keep mixture from becoming sticky. Serve in a heated serving dish with parsley sprinkled on top. Serve with heated cream on the side. Serves 2.

FINNAN HADDIE

3 pounds finnan haddie
1 quart milk
¼ cup onions, minced
¼ cup green pepper, chopped
10 tablespoons clarified butter (see Chapter 17)

¼ cup pimientoes, chopped
½ cup flour
2 cups cream
1 cup bread crumbs
Salt and pepper to taste

Preheat oven to 350°F. Poach finnan haddie in milk (see Poaching, Chapter 15) until fish separates easily. Drain and save the liquid. Flake fish, removing any bones. Arrange fish in a baking dish. Sauté onion and green pepper in 2 tablespoons butter until tender, approximately 5 to 10 minutes. Add pimientoes and cook an additional 2 minutes.

Warm remaining butter over a very low flame, add flour and cook for 2 minutes. Slowly add cream and milk from poaching. Simmer until mixture is smooth and thickened. Add vegetable mixture, salt, and pepper. Pour over fish, sprinkle with bread crumbs and bake, approximately 20 to 30 minutes.

Crabs

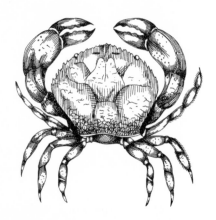

Crabs are crustaceans—part of a large group of aquatic arthropods—spineless animals with segmented bodies, jointed limbs, and a firm, crustlike outer shell. Crabs are found in oceans and bays, but some species are terrestrial for long periods of time. They have a large cephalothorax covered by a flat shell called a carapace from which five pairs of legs extend, the first pair bearing claws or pincers. Swimming crabs have flattened paddles at the ends of the hindmost pair of legs. The eyes are mounted on two short movable stalks and four antennae—two long, two short—cluster at the mouth. Bent under the cephalothorax is the small stomach which is flatter and wider in the female.

The female carries her eggs in her abdomen, where they are continually bathed by sea water. It takes two weeks for the eggs to hatch. Newly hatched crabs are free-swimming and it is several months before they become adults and live on the bottom. The female has a wide, rounded apron (the piece of shell that folds under the body toward the rear). Her claws are red at their tips before cooking. The male's apron is wide at one end, tapering to a slim base. The male's claws are blue stripes on white, without any red.

The claw meat of the crab is white, the body meat a darker color.

Soft-shelled crabs are not a distinct species. The name applies to any young crab caught between the shedding of an old shell and the hardening of the new and larger shell. The blue crab of the Atlantic is the most popular soft-shelled variety and lives in shallow bays and river channels. When found in fresh water, they are referred to as sweet-water crabs.

Stone crabs are also popular on the East Coast. The male stone crab has extremely large claws which are used in mating to capture a female. In most states, only one of the giant claws from the male may be taken.

King crabs, the largest edible crabs, can measure 9 feet wide. Once known as Japanese crabs and imported canned from Japan, king crabs became a major product of Alaska after World War II when the fishing beds came under U.S. supervision.

Dungeness crabs are large Pacific Coast variety—extremely delicious and flavorful.

Oyster crabs and mussel crabs are the size of a thumbnail with a smooth, shiny shell. Extremely sweet and delicate in flavor, the females of the species live inside the shells of East Coast oysters and mussels. Oyster crabs are limited in quantity.

LOCATION
Blue crabs are found all along the East Coast, from Massachusetts to the northern coast of South America. Chesapeake Bay is the richest source. Oyster crabs are found on the coasts of New England and Long Island. Stone crabs are found mainly around Miami, Palm Beach, Key West, and Cuba. King crabs are found in the North Pacific; the Dungeness along the Pacific Coast.

MARKET
Soft-shelled crabs are always sold fresh. The peak season is July and August. Buy the smallest crabs available; the flavor is better and the meat more tender than from larger ones. Buy 2 crabs per person.

Hard-shelled crabs are available all year, but are most plentiful during the summer months. Crabs are abundant and marketed in various forms: alive, whole, and freshly cooked or steamed, where they are taken and shipped in containers weighing ½ or 1 pound; as crab flakes—least expensive; in large chunks, called lump crabmeat—the best quality; and backfin, small chunks at a reasonable price. Large chunks of crabmeat are difficult to find because restaurants quickly buy out the wholesalers. Giant Alaskan king-crab legs are sold at high prices, but are very delicious. They are rarely shipped fresh but usually precooked and frozen in their shell or cleaned and canned. Stone crabs and oyster crabs are sold fresh. Buy ½ to ⅓ pound per person. Canned crabmeat sold in grocery stores is a combination of white and dark meat unless marked "white" or "deluxe." Crab flakes and chunks have a sweet flavor and can be eaten as purchased, with cocktail sauce and slices of lemon, baked, or cooked in omelettes, crepes, sauces, salads, bisque, bouillabaisse, fritters, patties, and chowders. Buy ¼ pound per person.

COOKING
One center section of a frozen, giant king crab leg is enough for one portion. There is no waste and it is ready to broil as purchased.

Oyster crabs must be cooked carefully. They are soft-shelled and are usually sautéed, salted, and eaten whole. Serve on buttered toast or with a delicately flavored fish.

The larger claws of stone crabs are served in the shell. The meat from the small claws are used in salads, omelettes, sauces, and the like. Boil water with salt. Add the stone-crab claws and cover. Boil for 20 minutes. Serve with melted butter and lemon wedges, or use any recipe calling for cooked crabmeat. For cracking the shells and getting out the meat, use nutcrackers and picks.

Cooking live hard-shelled crabs and removing the meat: Crabs must always be cooked alive. Rapidly boil 2 quarts of a liquid: plain water; mild bouillon; or water with ½ cup of vinegar, 2 tablespoons salt, and 1 teaspoon of cayenne pepper. Add the live crabs, cover, and boil 8 minutes to the pound (20 minutes for Dungeness crabs), or steam in a steamer for 30 minutes per pound. Crabs turn red when cooked. Remove crabs from water and allow to cool before removing the meat. Break off claws and legs from the body before cracking them open. Break off the piece of shell that folds under the body in the rear (the apron). Place a sharp knife into this new opening and force the shell apart. Pull the upper and lower halves of the shell apart with your fingers. Remove the spongy parts under the shell by cleaning it under running water (this is the digestive tract). The greenish fat and orange coral are edible.

Because the shells of the East Coast crabs have a hard covering on their outer edge, each half of the shell must be split along the longitudinal central crease with a sharp knife. Place the knife on the crease and push the knife through the shell with your hand. Remove the hard covering by cutting it away with a knife or kitchen shears. Use a pick to remove the meat.

Extract the meat of the Pacific dungeness by simply hitting each half of the crab firmly against a hard surface.

Soft-shelled crabs are purchased alive and usually cleaned and prepared by the dealer. To clean the crabs yourself, proceed as follows: With a sharp pointed knife, cut off the face behind the eyes. Remove the piece that folds under the body in the rear (the apron). Remove any spongy, digestive tract parts that can be seen. Lift all points along the sides with your fingers and clean out the gills. The greenish fat and orange coral are edible after the crab is cooked. Wash crabs in salted water and dry on paper towels. Sautéing is preferred, but soft-shelled crabs can also be broiled or deep-fat fried. The entire body can be eaten.

SAUTÉED SOFT-SHELLED CRABS

8 soft-shelled crabs, prepared for cooking (2 per person)
8 tablespoons clarified butter (see Chapter 17)

Flour (seasoned with salt and pepper)
Lemon slices

Place one crab at a time into a plastic bag with flour and gently shake until crab is coated. Sauté in hot butter until crisp on the edges, approximately 3 to 5 minutes on each side. Serve with lemon slices. Serves 4.

VARIATIONS
•   Remove cooked crabs from pan and sauté ½ to ¾ cup of slivered almonds until brown. Pour over crabs.
•   Add paprika to the flour, according to taste.

CRAB PAPRIKA

Note: It is best to use freshly cooked crabmeat for this recipe since the crabmeat should be served warm but must not be heated twice. Purchased precooked crabmeat would have to be reheated.

- 2 cups crabmeat, cooked, shelled, flaked and kept warm (do not chill)
- 1 teaspoon paprika
- ½ teaspoon powdered mustard
- ½ teaspoon pepper
- ⅛ teaspoon salt

- 5 tablespoons clarified butter (see Chapter 17)
- 2 tablespoons vinegar, red or white wine, or tarragon
- 1 hard-boiled egg, sliced
- 1 cucumber, sliced
- 1 tomato, cut in wedges

Heat paprika, mustard, pepper, salt and vinegar in butter, stirring constantly. Place crabmeat on a bed of lettuce. Pour sauce over shellfish. Garnish with slices of egg and cucumber and tomato wedges. Serves 2 large portions or 3 to 4.

CRAB WITH AVOCADO

- 1 large ripe avocado, peeled and pitted
- 1 clove garlic, minced
- 2 tablespoons lime juice or lemon juice

- 1 small onion, chopped
- 6 ounces cooked crabmeat, flaked
- ½ teaspoon salt
- 2 drops Tabasco sauce
- ½ cup sour cream

Mash avocado with a fork and add remaining ingredients. Blend well. Serve on toast or prepared toast squares.

Crayfish (Crawfish)

ROCK LOBSTER
SEA CRAWFISH
SPINY LOBSTER

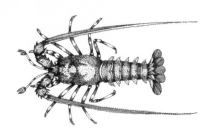

The crayfish is a freshwater and marine crustacean, an aquatic arthropod that has a firm, crustlike shell. The sea crayfish is called a spiny lobster or rock lobster that is structurally similar to the lobster. Freshwater crayfish are small, from 3 to 6 inches in length, and have a brownish green coloring. They can be found in streams, lakes, and ponds all over the world except in Africa. They are popular in Louisiana and the Mississippi river basin where a thick crayfish soup is a local specialty. They are also eaten in Oregon, Wisconsin, and Minnesota.

The saltwater spiny lobsters are similar to the true lobster but are actually distant relatives. They have spines protruding from the legs and body and lack large claws. They can grow to 4 feet in length but average from 9 to 12 inches. The meat of the broad tail is what is generally eaten and this is usually purchased frozen. The meat is firm, white, and savory.

Crayfish habitats have always been a matter of interest to aficionados. You can determine from what part of the world crayfish come by their stripes or spots and by the smoothness or roughness of the shell.

Color, too, is an indicator, but the color of the shell changes during the freezing process and makes it difficult to determine its origin by this alone.

LOCATION

Marine crayfish are found in Florida, Cuba, the Bahamas, and have a smooth shell, large yellow or white spots. The first segment of the tail is green. Western Australian crayfish have smooth shells, with small white dots. Most tail segments are reddish brown. Crayfish from Southern California and the west coast of Mexico have smooth shells with no spots or stripes, and their color varies from dark red to orange and brown. Crayfish from South Africa, New Zealand, and eastern Australia have rough shells with no spots, and they are chestnut-brown in color. Crayfish found in the Mediterranean and southwestern Europe have rough shells with white streaks and spots and are reddish tan in color. All crayfish are high in protein, vitamins, and minerals.

MARKET

Freshwater crayfish are available year round in most markets. They are marketed alive, cooked, in flakes, canned, and frozen. Freshwater crayfish are small. Buy as many as 1 dozen per person.

The most popular way of purchasing spiny lobsters is in the form of frozen tails. They can weigh from 4 ounces to more than 1 pound. Usually 2 medium-sized tails per person are sufficient. Live spiny lobsters are available in parts of Florida and California. Whole, cooked lobsters are also available, but generally the cooked meat is canned.

COOKING

Fresh crayfish must be alive before cooking. When cooked, the shell turns red and the meat tastes like true lobster meat. They can be cooked and eaten like lobsters (see Lobster). Spiny lobster tails can be boiled or broiled in the shell.

Broiling: Two methods:

1. Cut the membrane on the underside of a spiny lobster tail with cooking shears or a sharp knife. Bend the shell backward to prevent curling during cooking. Place on a broiler pan flesh side up.
2. Or remove the meat from the shell

before broiling. Cut the shell along the back to the tail flippers with kitchen shears or by running a knife along the shell, cutting through the shell only. Lift the meat out of the shell gently, leaving the flippers' end attached, if possible, and lay the meat on top of the shell.

Place tails on a broiler pan and brush with melted butter or any of the butters for fish. Broil in a preheated broiler, 4 inches under the flame 1 minute per ounce. Serve with melted butter and lemon wedges.

Boiling: For 6 tails, boil 2 quarts water with ⅓ cup salt. Place frozen tails in the water. Cover and simmer for 10 to 15 minutes after the water has returned to boiling. Remove and cut tails in half lengthwise. Serve with melted butter and lemon wedges.

Croaker

DRUM (sheepshead, spot)
WEAKFISH
WHITING

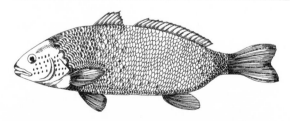

Croaker is a member of the abundant and diverse family of marine and freshwater fish called *Scianenidae,* that includes the drums (sheepshead), weakfish and whitings. The croaker's body is elongated and compressed, with spiny fins. It is a gluttonous, carnivorous fish that feeds on the bottom. With the exception of weakfish, the croaker has very sensitive chin barbels that help it to locate its prey. It has canine teeth. The dorsal fin is deeply notched or divided into two fins. The flesh is lean, white, and very tender with an excellent flavor and very few bones. The croaker's distinguishing characteristic is the grunting sound produced by most of the species. The sound is produced by vibrating muscles against the strained air bladder which acts as a resonance chamber.

DRUM

The *black drum* is the loudest of all and its musical sounds can be heard above the water's surface. The drum has a tendency to stand on its head with the tail visible above the water level. It sucks up food which is usually clams, crushing the shells with its head. It is olive in color, with long indented dorsal fins, a mouth overhung by a rounded snout, and a humped back. The flesh of the drum is fatty and it can weigh from ½ to 150 pounds. The *spot* is the smallest drum and the *sheepshead* is a freshwater drum, most popular in the South where it is called the *gaspergou*.

WEAKFISH

The weakfish has especially fragile flesh that can be torn easily. The coloration of the most common weakfish is silver, darker on the back with many small, irregular dark blotches, sometimes appearing as lines running downward and forward. The fins are either yellow or dusky and sometimes speckled.

WHITING

Whiting includes: kingfish, sea mink, and silver hake. These fish are slender, dark gray in color with silver undersides. Their flesh is very soft and fragile. They average ¾ to 4 pounds, but the kingfish can weigh as much as 75 pounds.

LOCATION

Croakers like shallow sandy waters in balmy seas. They are found on the Atlantic Coast in New England, Long Island, Virginia, the Carolinas, Florida, and the Gulf of Mexico.

Freshwater croakers are found in lakes and streams from the Great Lakes to Texas, in the Great Plains, Appalachian Mountain valleys, and throughout California.

MARKET

Croakers are available year round. Small croakers are usually sold whole and the large sizes are sold as fillets, fresh and frozen.

The peak of the season for the sheepshead drum in Louisiana is March and in the Midwest during May and June. The smallest catch available is during November through January. Sheepshead are available whole or in fillets.

The peak of the season for whitings is spring and fall. They are generally sold whole at ½ to 1½ pounds. The larger whitings are filleted. Frozen whiting is very popular in fast-food restaurants, served as fish and chips. Whiting is also available smoked and salted.

COOKING

Panfish are excellent sautéed. Larger croakers are excellent baked, filleted and fried, or broiled. Croakers are an extremely lean fish and need frequent basting during the cooking process (except for the drums).

- Serve croakers with: brown butter, lemon butter, or with any fish sauce.
- Whiting has lean and fragile flesh and does not cook well on a grill. It is best to prepare it whole. Poach in a milk and water bouillon with a pinch of salt.
- Sheepshead tends to be coarse in most cases. Small ones can be baked successfully, but large ones are best in chowders. Chunks can be broiled and have a texture and taste similar to lobster.

Eel

Eel is a common name for the family *Anguilla*, one species of which inhabits North American waters. The eel is characterized by a long, tubular body—greenish brown or yellowish brown in color—and long, continuous dorsal, caudal, and anal fins. It has no pelvic fins but is well adapted for wriggling in mud and through crevices. The head is small with small teeth. The skin is smooth and the scales are placed obliquely, some at right angles. The scales are embedded so well into the surface of the skin that they are hardly noticeable. The air bladder has an open duct to the throat. The flesh is oily, richly flavored, and very tender.

All American and European eels are hatched in the ocean south of Bermuda. They then migrate some 3,000 to 4,000 miles to the localities inhabited by their parents. This journey can take as long as three months or more. The American eel returns to freshwater after reaching one year of age and achieving a length of 3 inches. It is a small version of the adult and is called an *elver*. The European eel remains in the ocean for three years, but when it enters freshwater it travels further than the elver— as far as the inland streams of Switzerland.

The female reaches a length of 4 feet and swims farther inland than the male who reaches a length of 2 feet. They stay in freshwater for as long as 5 to 20 years.

The growing eel is a scavenger and a gluttonous eater, feeding on both dead and living animals. In its search for food, it travels over short distances of land in search of frogs and lizards. It is usually nocturnal in habit and rests during the day. As the eel matures sexually the appetite subsides; it eventually stops eating altogether and returns to the Atlantic spawning ground where it reproduces and dies.

LOCATION
The young eel enters American fresh water from the Gulf of Mexico to the St. Lawrence River. New York and New Jersey provide large catches that come from Lake Ontario and the tributaries of the St. Lawrence.

MARKET
The peak of the season for fresh eel is the late fall, but live eels are available year round in fish markets that maintain cold-water tanks. Eels are also sold by the pound, already prepared for cooking. Eels canned in a jelly, smoked, or kippered can be purchased in gourmet stores.

COOKING
Eel must be skinned before cooking. Usually the head is hung on a nail to make skinning easier. With a sharp knife, cut the skin

around the head. Pull off the skin with the aid of pliers. Cut along the bone from head to tail. Using a clean towel, take hold of the flesh and pull it from the bone. Cut the eel into 3-inch pieces and remove the intestines with a knife or fork. The flesh is oily and lends itself to many ways of preparation.

- Broil the pieces with rosemary, thyme, or sweet basil blended with 1 teaspoon of olive oil. Serve with lemon juice and freshly ground pepper. Mild sauces for oily fish can be used.
- Pan-fried smoked eel, chopped into small pieces, is considered a delicacy.
- Serve canned eel on a bed of lettuce or other greens with some sliced sweet onions, topped with mayonnaise or other cold dressing.
- Eel makes excellent chowder.

FRIED EEL

---

3 pounds eel, skinned, boned, and cut crosswise into 3-inch pieces
3 tablespoons brandy

¾ cup freshly squeezed lemon juice
Frying batter

Marinate eel in brandy and lemon juice for at least 1 hour. Drain eel and dry with paper towels. Coat with frying batter (see Deep-fat Frying, Chapter 12). Fry in deep fat until crisp. Drain and serve with any sauce. Serves 4.

BARBECUE SAUCE FOR EEL

(See Charcoal Broiling, Chapter 2.)

2 pounds eel, skinned, boned, and cut crosswise into 3-inch pieces
5 tablespoons powdered mustard

½ teaspoon paprika
7 drops Tabasco sauce
½ teaspoon salt
5 tablespoons boiling water
2 teaspoons olive oil

Combine mustard, paprika, Tabasco, and salt. Stir in boiling water and mix well. Add olive oil and blend thoroughly.

EEL CHOWDER

---

2 small eels, skinned, boned, and cut crosswise, into 1-inch pieces and, soaked in salted water for 10 minutes
2 onions, quartered
3 leeks, whites only, coarsely chopped
6 tablespoons butter (clarified preferred, see Chapter 17)
1 quart boiling water

1 cup spinach, minced
1 cup fresh lettuce minced (any kind)
½ cup bread crumbs
3 egg yolks, beaten gently without forming bubbles
⅔ cup warm heavy cream
Pinch nutmeg
Salt and pepper to taste

Sauté onions and leeks in 3 tablespoons of butter for 5 minutes. Add boiling water and eel. Bring to a boil and simmer for 30 minutes. Remove eel and keep warm on a warming plate or in a low heated oven. Put liquid through sieve and save liquid. Sauté spinach and lettuce in 2 tablespoons butter for 5 minutes, stirring constantly. Add ¼ cup of reserved liquid and bread crumbs. Blend well. Add this mixture to rest of the reserved liquid. Simmer for 10 minutes. Remove from heat and gradually add egg yolks; add cream and heat. Add eel, 1 tablespoon butter, salt, pepper, pinch of nutmeg. Serve with crackers. Serves 6.

Flatfish

SOLE (turbot)
FLOUNDER (blackback, dab, fluke, gray sole, halibut, plaice, winter flounder, yellowtail)

Flatfish is a common name for any member of the exclusive and widespread order *Pleuronectiformes,* which contains over 600 species. Of those species 130 are American, including dab, flounder, halibut, plaice, sole, and turbot. Flatfish are divided into two groups: the sole families *Soleidae, Cynoglossidae,* and *Achiridae;* and the flounder families *Bothidae* and *Pleuronectidae.*

The transparent young are bilaterally symmetrical. The body compresses and one "eye" migrates to the other side of the head; depending on the species, it moves to the right or left side, and the fish lies on its blind side with the eye side up.

Flattened body form is characteristic of all flatfish. This form is well suited to living on the bottom of the ocean where they feed on invertebrates, worms, and crustaceans. The entrails are encompassed by a very small rib cavity. The adults have one dorsal and anal fin, both without spines. The flesh is lean and mild-flavored.

SOLE FAMILY

In America, the name sole is used for any white-fleshed fish that is sold as fillets. The consumer usually has only a vague idea what fish he or she is buying and eating. Fillets that are sold as sole are usually members of the flounder family (dab, gray sole, lemon sole, yellowtail, winter flounder).

The American sole is generally too small and bony to be used as food fish. There are several species with mouths that appear to be twisted with few teeth or none at all. Their tiny eyes are set very close together. These fish are found in warm, shallow, sandy, and muddy waters. There is only one species of turbot in American waters. Its flesh is firm, white, and delicious. The average weight is 2 pounds.

The European sole grows to 2 feet in length and is shipped to the United States frozen. Its flavor is different from that of the fillets passed off as sole in the United States.

FLOUNDER FAMILY

There are over 500 species in the flounder family. They are characterized by their delicate texture. Flounder have tightly compressed oval or elliptical bodies, head that seem twisted, large eyes, and teeth. The Atlantic flounder is a dark, sandy gray with a white belly. The two eyes are close together on top of the head. The Pacific flounder is more brightly colored. All flounder can change their coloring to match their surroundings. Flounder migrate to breed in deeper waters during the winter. They average ¼ pound to 5 pounds.

Gray sole is considered the best flavored.

Lemon sole is the next best flavored.

Blackback is the meatiest flounder, with a very thick body.

Yellowtail is thin-bodied, but has a delicious flavor.

Dab has a thick underside and upperside with very few bones. Dab is sweet-flavored with a distinguishable texture.

Plaice, or sand dab weighs up to 14 pounds and grows to a length of 30 inches.

Fluke, or summer flounder is a meaty fish with white, sweet-flavored flesh. It can grow to 25 pounds but the average is from 1 to 5 pounds.

Halibut is the largest of all flatfish. It resembles a gigantic flounder with sharp, strong teeth in a large mouth. The firm flesh has a white, translucent appearance and is extremely flavorful. Halibut is a voracious eater of other fish and prefers cold waters. The Atlantic halibut averages 20 to 100 pounds; the Pacific halibut weighs up to 60 pounds. Halibut have been found to weigh as much as 600 pounds, the female usually outweighing the male.

The *chicken halibut* is rare, but can be found occasionally on both coasts weighing 5 to 10 pounds. The fishing season for halibut and the size of the catch is controlled by the International Pacific Halibut Commission. There is no control on the Atlantic Coast.

LOCATION

Flatfish are plentiful in both the Atlantic and Pacific oceans.

MARKET

They are available year round, whole, in fillets, steaks, and chunks; smoked, kippered, and frozen.

- Fluke has a peak season during the summer.
- Halibut, because of regulations on the Pacific Coast, is available fresh from May to the middle of July. Halibut is sold mainly as steaks and are very popular frozen. Halibut cheeks are occasionally sold (see Salmon in this Dictionary).
- When purchasing turbot, choose a large fish with very white underside and a meaty feel to the fillets.

- Buy flatfish fillets of ½ pound per person.
- European sole is imported frozen from England, Belgium, the Netherlands, and Denmark and is very expensive.

COOKING

Small flatfish are excellent panfish and whole fish or fillets can be prepared any way you desire to cook them. Serve with Hollandaise sauce or lemon butter.

- Flatfish is not usually turned when broiled.
- Fillets can be poached in a white wine, red wine, or champagne bouillon. Care must be taken not to overcook the fillets because they can be overdone in a few minutes.

- Halibut steaks are good poached in a milk-and-water bouillon with a pinch of salt.
- Deep-fat frying fillets of flatfish is not recommended because they cook so quickly and will resemble sawdust if overcooked. Always dredge them with flour, dip in a mixture of well-beaten eggs and milk, then roll in bread crumbs, corn flakes, corn meal, or cracker crumbs. Make sure the fillets are thoroughly covered (see Deep-fat Frying, Chapter 12). Serve with parsley that has been dipped into hot fat and fried for 2 minutes until crisp, Béarnaise sauce, lemon wedges, or tartar sauce.
- Any sauce can be used with flatfish.
- Wrap fillets around cooked asparagus tips. Poach in a water-milk bouillon (see Poaching, Chapter 15). Serve with a mild sauce or lemon wedges.

POACHED FLOUNDER FILLETS

---

2 large or 4 small flounder fillets
10 clams, cleaned and steamed, and left in the shell

10 mussels, cleaned and steamed, and left in the shell

Prepare fillets for poaching in salted water (see Poaching, Chapter 15). They take only 3 or 4 minutes to cook, so prepare the following béchamel sauce first. A few min-utes before sauce is finished, poach fish and pour finished sauce over cooked fish, garnishing with mussels and clams. Serves 4.

SAUCE

2 tablespoons onion, minced
2 tablespoons carrots, minced
8 tablespoons clarified butter (see Chapter 17)
3 tablespoons flour

1 cup milk
Salt and pepper to taste
1 cup shrimp, pounded to a paste
4 tablespoons cream
Pinch cayenne pepper

Sauté onion and carrots in 2 tablespoons butter until tender, approximately 10 minutes. Remove vegetables from the pan and set aside, leaving as much butter as possible. Add 2 more tablespoons butter and simmer for 20 minutes over very low heat. Combine shrimp paste with 4 tablespoons butter and press through a sieve.

Strain milk sauce to remove onion and carrots. Add cream and heat until well blended. Remove from heat and add shrimp-and-butter mixture. Blend a pinch of cayenne pepper into sauce and pour over poached fillets.

FILLET SOLE MEUNIÈRE

Dredge flatfish fillets in flour. Use a plastic bag with a small amount of flour added. Put the fillets, one at a time, into the bag and gently shake until the fish is coated with flour.

Sauté quickly (see Sautéing, Chapter 12) in half butter and half oil combination until brown and cooked. Turn once during cook-ing. Salt and pepper to taste. Remove fish to a hot platter, pour juices from pan over fish, and sprinkle with lemon juice.

VARIATION

Additional butter can be used: Anchovy butter, brown butter, or lemon butter.

FLATFISH FILLETS STUFFED WITH CRABMEAT

2 large or 4 small fillets	3 drops Tabasco sauce
1 small onion, minced	1 tablespoon sherry
3 tablespoons butter	2 tablespoons grated Swiss cheese
2 tablespoons flour	¼ teaspoon salt
1 cup milk	White pepper
¼ pound crabmeat chunks	Bread crumbs, approximately ¼ cup
½ teaspoon dry mustard	Paprika
½ teaspoon Worcestershire sauce	

Preheat oven at 375°F. Sauté onion in melted butter until tender, approximately 4 minutes. Stir in flour and cook for 2 minutes. Gradually add milk, stirring constantly until consistency is smooth and thickened. Set this white sauce aside. In a separate bowl combine mustard, Worcestershire sauce, Tabasco sauce, sherry, grated cheese, salt, pepper, and crabmeat. Add ½ cup of white sauce and blend well. Divide mixture evenly on all fillets and roll fillets, securing ends with toothpicks, if necessary. Place fish on an oiled baking dish. Pour remaining white sauce over fish. Sprinkle evenly with bread crumbs and paprika. Dot with butter. Bake in oven for approximately 20 minutes. Serves 2. This recipe can be doubled or tripled without any change in flavor.

HALIBUT FINGERS

Halibut steaks, ¾-inch thick
Flour

1 egg, beaten
Bread crumbs

Cut steaks into finger-size pieces. Roll halibut in flour, dip into egg, and in bread crumbs. Deep fry (see Deep-fat Frying, Chapter 12).

Serve with lemon wedges, remoulade sauce, or tartar sauce.

HALIBUT STEAKS

1 2-pound steak, 1-inch thick
1 teaspoon salt
1 teaspoon pepper
1 tablespoon paprika

Flour
Butter
Oil

Put flour, salt, pepper, and paprika into a plastic bag. Place halibut into bag and shake gently. Coat fish evenly with flour. Sauté in half butter and half oil combination.
Serves 4.

VARIATIONS

• Remove halibut from pan and keep warm on a warming plate or a very low oven. Add 1 cup sour cream to the pan juices. Heat only; do not boil (the sour cream will lose its thickness if boiled). Pour over fish. Serve with rice or noodles.
• First dip the halibut steak in lemon or lime juice, next in flour, then back in juice, then in unseasoned bread crumbs. Sauté.
• After sautéing, remove halibut from pan. Keep warm on a warming plate or a very low oven. Combine ⅛ cup Worcestershire sauce, ¼ cup dry white wine or sherry, 2 teaspoons prepared mustard, 1 teaspoon dry mustard in the pan juices. Boil for 1 minute and pour over cooked fish.
• While sautéing, add 1 teaspoon dried tarragon or 1 tablespoon fresh tarragon.
• After sautéing, remove fish. Keep warm on a warming dish or a very low oven. Add ½ cup dry white wine to the pan juices. Boil for 1 minute and pour over cooked fish.

Flounder   see Flatfish

Herring

ALEWIFE
ANCHOVIES
SARDINES
SHAD

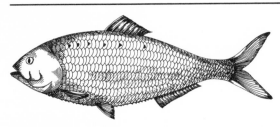

Herring is a common name for members of a large family *Clupeidae,* with 150 species of freshwater and marine food fish that includes alewife, anchovies, sardines, and shad.

Herring swim in large schools. In the northern hemisphere schools swim in a counterclockwise direction and in the southern hemisphere, clockwise. Some schools have been seen covering a 6-mile diameter.

Herring feed on plankton, small plants, and small animals. All members of the herring family are bony and have a rich, oily flesh with a strong flavor. During the spawning season, the flesh is very sweet, the opposite of most other fish. Some species spawn on the sea bottom. The two-year-old, 6-inch young of these species are known as sperling. Others spawn in shallow waters; shad and alewife are the best known anadromous types that spawn in large rivers.

ALEWIFE
Alewife include the branch herring and the blueback. Like the shad, they are ocean dwellers and migrate into freshwater to spawn. Alewife have short heads and large

eyes. Their color is bluish on top with silvery sides and a dark stripe along the rows of scales. Behind the opercle is a black spot. Their weight averages ½ pound and they grow 8 to 10 inches in length.

ANCHOVIES
The nose of the anchovy looks like a pig's snout and the mouth is set back a distance on the underside of the head. Anchovies are bluish in color with silvery sides. They can grow to 4 inches in length. Spanish and Italian anchovies, caught in the Mediterranean, are cured by a fermentation process. Other European anchovies are small and no fermentation process is involved. These are sold as Norwegian or Swedish anchovies or sardines.

HERRING
Herring have an oblong or elongated body, usually quite flat laterally. They are a deep blue-silver with a line of dark spots above and behind the gill area and a deeply forked tail. Herring have smooth, unscaled heads and small mouths with small teeth. Freshwater herring have silver bellies, blue backs, and occasionally a golden sheen. Herring seldom exceed 1 pound or 1 foot in length.

SARDINES
In the United States, young herring 3 to 4 inches long are called sardines and canned

in New Brunswick and Maine. Other countries use any tiny fish with a frail bone structure (France, Spain, and Portugal use the pilchard). Most authorities believe the word sardine comes from the island of Sardinia where fish were packed in the familiar tight arrangement. Sardines are very nutritious, being high in protein, minerals, and vitamins.

Processing of sardines:

1. Herring are pumped aboard a cannery carrier. During this process the scales are removed. (The scales are used in cosmetics, artificial pearls, and other products.)
2. Herring are salted as they come out of the pump.
3. They are carefully inspected by state officials at the dock and sent to the cannery.
4. When the approved herring arrive at the cannery, they are washed and cooked. After heads and tails are removed, they are packed into cans.
5. Sauces and oils are then added and the cans firmly sealed.
6. The cans are sterilized and go through a final cooking process.
7. A sample is inspected for flavor and appearance before shipping to markets.

SHAD

Shad is the largest member of the herring family, averaging 1½ to 6 pounds. Shad live in the ocean but breed in fresh water and are considered freshwater fish. During the spring they migrate upstream, eating no food as they ascend rivers and streams.

Their bodies are compressed in shape and bluish on top with silvery sides and forked tails. Shad have dark spots behind their gills that sometimes spread onto the body as lighter spots. The upper jaw has a deep, sharp notch at the tip and the adults are toothless. Shad are delicious with a sweet flavor, but extremely bony. The roe of shad is considered a delicacy, especially in the United States.

LOCATION

Alewife are found from the Gulf of St. Lawrence to the Carolinas, and from the Bay of Fundy to Florida.

Anchovies are found in warm waters all over the world.

Herring is found around the world. In North America they are caught mainly in Lake Erie and Lake Ontario and from Labrador to the coast of Florida.

Sardines first appear in Massachusetts in early spring. Later they are found in Maine, the Bay of Fundy, Nova Scotia, and on the West Coast.

Shad: East Coast shad have been severely overfished, but they were successfully introduced into Pacific waters from California to southeastern Alaska and are shipped to the East. Shad run in North Carolina in February and March; in Chesapeake Bay in March; in New Jersey and the Hudson River in April; and in Florida in December. Shad are also found in the Mississippi River and the Great Lakes.

MARKET

Alewife: The peak season is January to June. Fresh alewife is difficult to find unless you live near the catch. Alewife is marketed salted, cured in vinegar, smoked, kippered, canned, or salted in brine. The roe can also be purchased in cans.

Anchovies: Available canned, salted in brine, smoked and kippered, or dried and salted.

Herring are marketed weighing less than 1 pound. There isn't a great demand for fresh herring; they are most popular dried, smoked, and kippered in fillets. Salted or pickled herring from Holland and Germany are sold in brine. Herring is sold as red herring, kippers (herring preserved by salting and drying or smoking) and bloaters (older and fat herring preserved by lightly salting and smoking or drying). They can be purchased in cans, but other forms are superior.

Sardines: Sold all seasons in cans—salted, smoked, spiced, or in oils or sauces. Sardines in olive, soybean, peanut or cottonseed salad oils are packed in cans of about 3¼ ounces. Those in tomato and mustard sauces are packed in 3¼ and 12 ounce sizes. Fresh sardines are also available but are not in great demand.

Shad: January through May is the peak of the season. Shad are sold whole in weights of 1½ to 8 pounds. "Cut shad" refers to the whole female without roe; "buck" is a male with milt. Shad can also be purchased as fillets, which usually come from the female because the meat is larger, fatter, and juicier. Kippered, smoked, and boned fillets are available canned. At the end of their season shad roe becomes plentiful and is sold in pairs.

COOKING

All members of the fresh herring family can be pan fried and broiled. Serve with lemon butter, remoulade sauce, or tartar sauce.

- Score the herring on each side. Spread a thin layer of French or English mustard over the herring. Top with a pinch of cayenne pepper and sprinkle with unseasoned bread crumbs. Broil (see Broiling, Chapter 10), basting with melted butter.
- Smoked herring must be soaked for a few hours to eliminate some of the smoky flavor. Soak in water, half water and half milk, or in white wine.
- Kippers should be placed skin side up in a baking pan. Spread melted butter mixed with oil on top and warm in a moderate oven or broiler, being careful not to dry them by overcooking.
- Herring in brine, which is delicious, must be soaked in cold water, changing the water periodically for 24 hours to remove the brine. After soaking, cut off the head, split the body in half, bone and skin it, then cook in any way for herring.
- Bake boned shad in a well-oiled baking pan at 400°F for 10 minutes per pound. Serve plain with a sprinkling of salt and pepper or with a wine sauce.
- Because of its size, fresh shad is excellent stuffed and baked. Serve with herb butter or lemon butter. (Special care is needed to bone shad if preparing fillets. See Filleting, Chapter 6).
- Shad roe is excellent fried. Care must be taken not to overcook shad roe.

SAUCE FOR SMOKED HERRING

¼ cup French or English style mustard	1 tablespoon vinegar, white, cider, or tarragon
¼ cup sweet brown German mustard	Salt and pepper to taste
2 teaspoons sugar	1 tablespoon fresh dill, minced
2 tablespoons oil	

Combine mustards and blend in sugar. Add oil, a few drops at a time, beating constantly until thick and smooth. Gradually add enough vinegar to thin sauce slightly. Season with salt and pepper and more sugar or vinegar if desired. Blend in dill immediately before serving. Serve with herring on the side. Makes ½ cup.

SARDINE SALAD

2 3¼-ounce cans sardines, chilled
4 hard-cooked eggs, sliced
½ cup sharp cheese, coarsely chopped

1 cucumber sliced
1 tomato, cut in wedges
   Slice sweet onion for each serving

Combine all ingredients. Serve on a bed of greens with Russian dressing. Serves 2.

SAUTÉED SHAD ROE

2 pairs shad roe
4 tablespoons clarified butter (see Chapter 17)

Flour
Salt and pepper

Carefully coat roe with flour. Sauté (see Sautéing, Chapter 12) in butter in a covered pan for approximately 8 to 10 minutes, depending on size. Turn, cover, and sauté an additional 5 to 7 minutes. Salt and pepper when cooked. Serve with lemon wedges. Serves 2.

SHAD ROE BROILED WITH BACON

3–4 pairs shad roe (approximately 1½ pounds)
     Boiling water

1 tablespoon melted butter
8 slices bacon

Preheat broiler. Place roe in a saucepan and add enough boiling water to cover. Simmer for 5 minutes. Drain. Place roe on a broiler pan. Baste with butter and cover roe with bacon. Broil 4 inches below flame for 8 to 10 minutes, or until roe is a golden brown. Serve with lemon wedges and tartar sauce. Serves 4.

VARIATION
Add a pinch of rosemary to the boiling water while simmering roe.

Lobster

The lobster is a marine crustacean, an aquatic arthropod with a firm, crustlike shell. Lobster is one of the largest shellfish and contains high quantities of proteins, minerals, and vitamins.

The lobster has five pairs of legs, each pair connected. The first two legs, near the head, have large claws surrounded by blunt teeth that are capable of crushing the shells of clams and other shellfish. Lobsters also attack live fish and large gastropods. The other legs are used for crawling over the ocean floor, but the tail and abdomen are the main swimming apparatus. Making scooping motions, the lobster moves with great speed in water, although it is quite clumsy on land.

Connected to the sides of the body and base of the legs are 20 pairs of gills. The gills are protected by the shell (or carapace) that covers the back and sides of the body and consists of the 14 segments of the cephalothorax and the 7 segments of the muscular abdomen. The shell is shed regularly and replaced by a new one as the lobster grows in size. The lobster is dark bluish-green when alive, turning the familiar bright "lobster red" when cooked.

There are two pairs of long, slender antennae and six pairs of mouth parts. Attached to the abdominal sections are small swimmerets, or flippers. The female lobster's tail is wider than the male's. The female roe, which is delicious and very desirable, can be found in the lobster that has thin, wispy, featherlike flippers at the top of the lobster tail. The male has long and spiny flippers.

The eggs are attached to the female for almost a year until they hatch and become free-swimming larvae. During their first year, they molt approximately 17 times, then take on adult form and remain on the bottom. It takes about 5 years for a lobster to reach an average weight of 3 pounds. In deeper waters, they can grow to a weight of 20 pounds.

Lobsters are captured in slatted wooden traps. Although they have been protected by law, they are still an endangered species. The spiny or rock lobster are actually crayfish (see Crayfish).

LOCATION

Lobsters are found in the North and Middle Atlantic: in deep waters in winter and shallow waters during the summer. Most of the catch in the United States comes from the New England coast. Lobsters from Florida and California are really crayfish (see Crayfish).

MARKET

Lobsters are available all year but are more plentiful in summer when they are in shallow waters. The season is May through December in the Northeast: October through March on the West Coast. Lobster is marketed alive, cooked in the shell and as cooked, shelled meat. When picked up, live lobsters should curl the tail segment underneath the body. Never buy one whose tail hangs down. The average weights are 1 to 3 pounds.

CLASSIFICATION OF LOBSTERS BY WEIGHT

Chickens	¾ to 1 pound
Quarters	1¼ pounds
Large	1½ to 2¼ pounds
Jumbo	over 2½ pounds

The smaller the lobster the better the texture and taste. A 2½-pound lobster yields approximately 2 cups of shelled meat.

When choosing a live lobster in a restaurant always pick up the lobster. If it feels very light or if there is a slight trace of foam at the mouth, don't take it because it probably has been there too long.

Lobsters cooked in the shell are also sold by the pound. Purchase one that has a bright red coloring. When the tail is pulled straight it should return quickly to its rolled-up position. Cooked, shelled lobster meat is available fresh and frozen. Canned meat is available in cans of 6, 14, and 16 ounces. Most canned lobster comes from Canada. The frozen lobster tails that are available actually come from crayfish (see Crayfish).

COOKING

Purchase whole lobster in 1- to 1½-pound sizes per person; canned meat, ¼ pound per person. Fresh lobster must be alive and active at the time of cooking. It can be boiled, steamed, broiled, sautéed or used in a bouillabaisse or chowder. Lobster shrinks more than any other seafood during cooking. Cooked lobster, both in the shell and canned, can be baked, broiled, used in a bisque, bouillabaisse, fritters, patties, or as a cocktail served with cocktail sauce and lemon wedges.

Boiling is the easiest way to prepare lobster. In a large lobster pot, rapidly boil salted water, using 1 tablespoon salt to each quart of water (for the average 1- to 1½-pound lobster you need 3 quarts of water); or use a bouillon made of 4 quarts water, 2 small bay leaves, 1 chopped carrot, 1 chopped onion, 1 sliced lemon, 1 tablespoon salt; ¼ teaspoon pepper; and 3 sprigs fresh parsley. Pick up the lobster behind the head and plunge it into the pot head first. Lobster claws are usually pegged to prevent them from opening, but if they are not, be careful when handling. If you prefer not to put it into the water alive, you can sever the spinal cord with a heavy, sharp knife, inserting it between the tail and body segments and cutting downward quickly. There are other theories about cooking lobster. One is to put the lobster into warm water and bring it to a boil. The lobster supposedly falls asleep or the nerves are deadened in warm water and it feels no pain when the water boils.

Cover the pot tightly. Boil a 2-pound lobster for 10 minutes; under 2 pounds, boil for 7 minutes. Or, after the lobster is plunged into boiling water, cover and simmer 5 minutes for the first pound and 3 minutes for each additional pound.

After cooking, remove lobster from water; lay it on its back and split it in half, starting at the head, with a heavy, sharp knife, hitting the knife with a mallet or hammer. Remove the stomach and the black intestinal stringlike vein that runs from head to tail. Remove the small sac behind the head. The green liver—or tomalley—and coral parts which are the female's roe are edible and delicious. Serve with melted butter and lemon wedges. If the meat is to be used for cooking; extract the meat with a fork, cracking claws with a nutcracker or mallet.

Broiling: Some markets will prepare lobster for broiling on request. To do it yourself, first sever the spinal cord of the lobster with a heavy, sharp knife, inserting it between the tail and body segment and cutting downward quickly. Lay the lobster on its back and split it in half with the knife, starting at the head, hitting the knife with a mallet or hammer. As with a boiled lobster, remove the stomach and the black intestinal vein, which runs from the head to the tail, and the small sac behind the head, but leave the green liver (tomalley) and coral (roe) which are edible and

delicious. Crack the claws with a nutcracker or mallet. Preheat broiler for approximately 10 minutes. Spread melted butter on each half of the lobster, and season with salt and pepper if desired. Place the lobster halves, flesh side up, on a broiler pan.

Broiling Time	
Less than 2 pounds	7 minutes
2 pounds	10 minutes
More than 2 pounds	12 to 15 minutes

Lobster must be basted frequently with melted butter while broiling. Serve with melted butter and lemon wedges.

HOW TO EAT LOBSTER IN THE SHELL
Use a small cocktail fork to extract the meat from the tail and body. Cut these chunks into bite-size pieces and dip in melted butter. Crack the claws with a lobster cracker or nutcracker and extract the meat with a cocktail fork. The little claws can be pulled off with the fingers and the small pieces of tasty meat can be sucked out.

Mackerel

ALBACORE
BONITO
TUNA

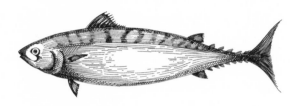

Mackerel is the common name for members of the family *Scombridae*. There are over 60 species, the most important being the tuna. The albacore and the bonito are members of the tuna family.

The tail of the mackerel is deeply forked and extremely narrow where it joins the body. Behind the anal and dorsal fins there are tiny finlets. The body is round and elongated and is almost scaleless, with a glossy metallic sheen. Steel blue is usually the dominant color. The jaws are lined with very sharp teeth. These fish are excellent swimmers. Smaller species must move constantly to keep fresh oxygenated water passing over the gills or they will suffocate. Because of their cylindrical shape, mackerel depend for movement on rapid oscillation of the caudal fin.

Mackerel swim in schools and feed mainly on herring, squid, and small crustaceans. They prefer warm waters and migrate back and forth between deep and shallow waters from winter to summer.

The flesh has a firm oily texture and a rich, savory flavor. Because of its texture and versatility, it is most frequently canned.

Mackerel (especially tuna) are high in animal protein, the B vitamins, calcium, phosphorous, iron, copper, and iodine.

SPANISH MACKEREL

Spanish mackerel have beautiful deep blue iridescent, elongated bodies with pointed heads. Some have bronze spots on silvery sides. They can weigh up to 75 pounds and, although popular, are very expensive.

BONITO

The bonito has a longer body than most other mackerel and has 21 spines in the dorsal fin. It can weigh up to 15 pounds. The Atlantic species is steel blue with dark, narrow, oblique stripes and a silver stomach. The California bonito is blue on the back and dusky on the sides, with black oblique stripes running in the opposite direction— upward and backward from the pectoral part of the body to the top edge of the caudal fin.

TUNA AND ALBACORE

The world stock of tuna is diminishing, and the number and size of catch are now government-controlled. Several different species of fish are sold as tuna: albacore, bluefin (the largest), skipjack, and yellowfin in the Pacific; horse mackerel, little tuna, and white bluefin in the Atlantic. The usual weight is 8 to 65 pounds, but tuna can grow as large as 1,600 pounds. The tuna is lightmeated. The albacore, which weighs up to 60 pounds, has the lightest meat and, when canned, it is labeled "white meat." All other canned species are labeled "light meat" tuna.

LOCATION
All species are abundant in the Atlantic, the Pacific, and the Indian oceans and in warm seas all over the world. The European species inhabit the Mediterranean. The Spanish mackerel is rare on the Pacific Coast, but can be found between San Diego and the Galapagos Islands.

MARKET

Spanish mackerel: The season is April to November for fresh fish, usually sold whole in weights averaging ¾ to 3 pounds, and in sizes up to 16 inches long. It is also marketed in fillets, frozen, smoked, kippered, salted, and canned. Larger mackerel are steaked.

Bonito: When available (during the summer), it is sold in thick steaks, but is usually found canned in chunks and flakes.

Tuna and albacore: The season for fresh tuna on the Atlantic Coast is from July to October and on the Pacific Coast from May to December. Fresh tuna and albacore are marketed as steaks. Tuna is packed in three different forms, which refer only to the size of the pieces in the can, not to the quality of the meat.

1. *Fancy or solid pack.* The most expensive, and consists of the best cuts of white albacore. Cans of 3½, 7 and 13 ounces contain 3 or 4 large pieces packed in oil, salt, and vegetable broth.

This form is used for recipes in which good appearance is necessary.

2. *Chunk Style.* Moderately priced; cans come in ¾, 6, 6½, and 12 ounces. The pieces are cut into the same size and packed in oil, salt, and vegetable broth. This form is used mainly for salads and sandwiches without any dressing, such as mayonnaise. Usually albacore meat.

3. *Flake and grated style.* Lower-priced than the others and available in cans of 6 and 11 ounces. The pieces are cut smaller than the chunk style and are packed in oil, salt, and vegetable broth. Excellent for sandwiches made with mayonnaise or other dressings and for canapes. This form is usually the darker meat from one or more of the species of mackerel other than albacore.

Specialty packs: Dietetic varieties are packed in distilled water. "Tonno" is solid meat packed in olive oil with double the quantity salt that is usually added to the other canned forms. Tuna is also available as baby food and tuna paste.

COOKING
The firm, oily flesh of fresh tuna lends itself to any cooking method. Most people prefer to remove the skin. However the skin can be left on while cooking and removed by the cook or the diner. When frying remove the skin first.

- Sauces for tuna: lemon butter, tartar sauce, curry sauce, tomato sauce, parsley sauce, Hollandaise sauce, or any sauce desired.
- Fresh dark meat of tuna tastes much like veal and should be broiled with butter.
- Poached albacore is delicious cooked in a court bouillon and served with

sweet-sour sauce, Béarnaise sauce, or oyster sauce. Cold, poached albacore can be served with an olive oil mayonnaise, Russian dressing or remoulade sauce.

- Canned tuna, albacore, bonito and mackerel are staples in casseroles with macaroni products, rice, potatoes or vegetables, and in sandwiches and salads. Unless the recipe indicates that canned fish should be drained, use the liquid in the cans because it is high in nutritive value.

MACKEREL

4 mackerel fillets	4 tablespoons clarified butter (see
Lemon or lime juice	Chapter 17)
Flour	

Prepare mackerel for sautéing (see Sautéing, Chapter 12). Dip fish into lemon juice and coat with flour. Fill a plastic bag with flour and coat one fillet at a time by putting into bag and shaking gently. Coat fish evenly with flour. Put the fillets on waxed paper until ready to cook. Meanwhile, prepare the following sauce:

SAUCE

2 cloves garlic, juiced	¼ cup scallions, white part only,
⅓ cup oil	minced
2 tablespoons lime or lemon juice	2 drops Tabasco sauce
⅓ cup fresh orange juice	

Combine all ingredients.

Sauté fish. When cooked, remove from pan. Add sauce to pan juices and heat. Pour over cooked fish. Garnish with lemon wedges. For a change in flavor add a pinch of ground coriander to the sauce. Serves 4.

MACKEREL WITH MUSTARD

1 whole mackerel, split for broiling	⅛ teaspoon fennel
2 tablespoons fresh parsley, chopped, or 1 tablespoon dried parsley	1 lemon, thinly sliced
2 ounces clarified butter (see Chapter 17)	2 tablespoons lemon juice
1 tablespoon mustard, French or English style	Salt and pepper to taste

Preheat broiler. Combine 1 ounce butter with parsley and brush mackerel well with butter mixture. Season with salt and pepper. Place mackerel skin side down on top of lemon slices in an oiled broiler pan. (See Broiling, Chapter 10.) Broil 2 inches below flame for 5 minutes. While broiling, combine all other ingredients. Pour mixture over mackerel and broil an additional 5 to 10 minutes. Serves 2.

HOT OR COLD TUNA SALAD

- *1* can (7 ounces, chunk style) tuna, drained and separated
- ¼ cup green onion, chopped
- ⅛ cup oil
- *10* snow peas
- *2* cups cooked rice, unseasoned
- *1½* tablespoons soy sauce
- *1* egg, beaten
- ½ can (5 ounces) water chestnuts, drained and chopped

In a frying pan, sauté onion in oil until tender, approximately 10 minutes. Add rice and soy sauce and cook for 5 minutes. Push rice to sides of pan. Put egg in center and scramble. Mix with rice. Combine all other ingredients with rice mixture. Heat, blending well. Serve either hot or cold on beds of lettuce. Serves 2.

TUNA SALAD

- *1* can (7 ounces) tuna, drained and separated into large chunks
- *1½* cups carrots, shredded
- *1* can (5 ounces) pineapple chunks, drained
- ¼ cup celery, sliced crosswise
- ¼ cup mayonnaise
- ⅛ cup seedless raisins
- ⅛ cup sunflower seeds
  Salad greens

Combine all ingredients except greens. Mix gently. Serve on greens (watercress, spinach, or lettuce). Garnish with sliced cucumber, onion, or tomato. Serves 2.

Mussel

The mussel is a bivalve mollusk, found in both fresh water (family *Unionidae*) and salt water (family *Mytilidae*). The two valves fit together tightly, protecting it from its deadly enemy, the starfish. The bluish black, slightly pear-shaped shell is very thin and rather soft with a faintly ribbed texture. Because the shell is so thin, there is more food per pound of mussels than either oysters or clams. Mussels are also the least expensive seafood. Mussel meat is a golden color and is tender and sweet.

The mussel moves, when it has to, by means of a muscular foot and feeds and breathes through two tubes called *siphons*. One tube sucks in water containing oxygen and food particles, the other expels water containing waste. A large mussel can filter up to 10 gallons of water daily. The mussel anchors itself to a solid object by a tassle of black threads called *byssus* that it secretes. Mussels generally remain stationary all their lives.

The popular blue mussel grows to 3 inches long and is found along the Atlantic Coast. The 6-inch horse mussel, which is usually seen only where it is caught inhabits

deep waters of the Atlantic and Pacific. The orange and yellow shells, called jingle shells, that are often found on beaches are related to the marine mussel.

Mussels have been artificially propagated in huge quantities to meet the great, worldwide demand.

LOCATION
Mussels are abundant in cooler waters of the Atlantic and Pacific oceans. The largest sources are Massachusetts, Connecticut, and Rhode Island. Pacific Coast mussels are occasionally quarantined during the peak season because they sometimes absorb poisonous pollutants. Freshwater mussels come from the middle United States and middle Europe.

MARKET
Live mussels must be tightly closed when purchased. If any are partially opened and do not close when handled, they are dead and must be discarded. There are usually 15 to 20 mussels per pound. Mussels are also available canned and smoked.

COOKING
Live mussels in the shell can be baked, boiled, broiled, sautéed, steamed, used in bouillabaisse or broth. Shucked mussels can be baked, broiled, deep-fat fried, pan fried, used in bisques, chowders, fritters, patties, pies, soups, or stews. Canned varieties can

be used in canapés or eaten right out of the can. Mussels must be cleaned well if the liquid in which they are cooked is to be served.

CLEANING MUSSELS

1. Use a stiff, preferably wire, brush to scrub the mussels clean under cold running water, and pull the beards off. The barnacles can be removed with a knife.

2. Place the mussels in a large pot or in the sink and cover with water.

3. Allow the mussels to stand for two hours so they spit out any sand left in the shell, or put a handful of flour in the water and leave overnight. The mussels eat the flour and at the same time clean themselves of sand. Clean again in the morning.

4. Throw away any mussels that float; they are not fit to eat. Also, if any shell feels excessively heavy, it is full of sand and must be discarded.

STEAMING MUSSELS

1. In a large pot, bring to a boil 1 inch of water, wine, or a mixture of both, and 1 teaspoon salt.

2. Place the cleaned mussels in the pot and cover.

3. Steam until the shells begin to open, approximately 3 minutes.

The mussels can be served as is with melted butter and lemon wedges or the meat can be removed from the shells for use in other recipes.

If raw mussels are needed in a recipe, open the shells as follows:

1. Clean as described above.

2. Look for the small hole where the beard is attached. Insert a paring knife into this opening and run the blade around the shell. The shell should open easily.

BOUILLON FOR STEAMED MUSSELS

1½ cups dry white wine	1 tablespoon celery seed
½ cup water	1 tablespoon dried dill or 2
2 tablespoons fresh parsley, chopped, or 1 tablespoon dried parsley	tablespoons fresh dill, chopped
2 tablespoons prepared mustard, French or English style	1 garlic clove, minced
1 tablespoon sugar	3 tablespoons clarified butter (see Chapter 17)

Combine all ingredients and bring to a boil. Add cleaned mussels and steam (see Steaming, Chapter 14). Strain bouillon and serve with mussels and toasted French or garlic French bread for dipping into liquid. Makes approximately 2 cups.

MUSSELS MARINIÈRE

2 quarts mussels, cleaned	⅛ teaspoon coarse pepper
1 large onion, chopped	1 cup dry white wine
3 sprigs fresh parsley	3 tablespoons fresh parsley, chopped, or 1½ tablespoon dried parsley flakes
Large pinch thyme leaves	
7 tablespoons clarified butter (see Chapter 17)	Salt to taste (optional)

In a saucepan deep enough to hold mussels, place onion, parsley, and thyme. Add mussels, 4 tablespoons butter, and pepper. Pour wine over mussels. Cover and steam over low heat until mussels open. Discard unopened mussels.

Place mussels into two large serving bowls. Add remaining butter and parsley to broth. Add salt, if desired. Pour broth over mussels. Serve with toasted plain or garlic French bread and dip bread into the broth. Serves 2.

MUSSEL SOUP

4 dozen mussels, cleaned	4 tablespoons oil
1 large onion, minced	1½ cups rice, uncooked
3 sprigs parsley	1 teaspoon salt
1 bay leaf	Pinch saffron
5½ cups water	Pinch pepper
3 leeks, minced (white parts only)	

In a deep saucepan, put in mussels, onion, parsley, bay leaf, and water. Cover and steam over low heat until mussels open. Remove mussels from pan, saving liquid, and keep warm either in the shell or shucked. Sauté leeks in oil until tender, approximately 3 to 5 minutes. Add liquid and bring to a boil. Add rice, salt, pepper, and saffron. Simmer until rice is cooked, about 30 minutes. Add mussels just before serving. Makes approximately 2½ quarts.

Oyster

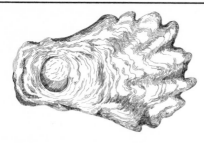

The oyster is a bivalve mollusk found in the shallow waters of bays and ponds, usually at the point where the salt in the water is lessened by the flow of fresh water.

The oyster's upper valve is flat, the lower one slightly bulged. The shell has a very rough and irregular surface. The opening and closing of the shell is controlled by one muscle that joins the two halves along one edge. Some shells are round, others flat.

The meat of the oyster is a dark gray-green and extremely succulent. There are many varieties of oysters. Most species are not large enough to use as food or, like the Japanese oyster, too large to eat on the half-shell. The common oyster we purchase and eat grows from 2 to 6 inches. Pearls come from a tropical species that grows up to 12 inches long. Even in the same waters, quantities of salt and copper vary from bed to bed, resulting in great differences in taste.

After a free-swimming larval state (the larvae are called *veligers*) the oyster attaches itself permanently by a sticky substance to rocks, shells, or roots. There is a hermaphroditic species that is born with a shell.

Oysters are an extremely rich source of protein, minerals, and vitamins. The nutritional balance of oysters is superior to that of most foods. Of the recommended daily amounts of the following nutrients, six oysters supply more than enough iron and copper; half the iodine; and one-tenth of the protein, calcium, magnesium, phosphorous, vitamins A, B, C, D, and G, thiamine, riboflavin, and niacin. Oysters contain more protein than milk. Only additional calories are necessary for a balanced meal. Because of their nutritional value, oysters are in great demand and cultivated artificially on both coasts. The beds are seeded with veligers or young sessile oysters called *spots*. These mature in 1½ years if harvested in warm waters; 4 to 5 years in cooler waters. They are constantly transplanted into different beds to improve flavor and stimulate growth.

LOCATION

Blue points and Rockaways come from Long Island; Coluits from Massachusetts; Lynnhavina from Virginia. Half the supply of Atlantic oysters comes from the Chesapeake Bay and Long Island. The rest come from Delaware, the Gulf Coast of Louisiana, and artificial beds in Maine and New Hampshire. Pacific oysters are found on the coast of Washington and Puget Sound.

MARKET

Oysters are most plentiful in September, but

the best oysters are available in October. They can be purchased alive in the shell, fresh and frozen shucked, prebreaded frozen, canned, canned stews and soups, smoked whole or sliced in cans.

ALIVE IN THE SHELL

The shells must be tightly closed when purchased. Those that are partially opened should close quickly when handled. If they don't, they are dead and not edible. Live oysters are sold generally by the dozen and can be kept for quite a while at 40°F.

Shucked oysters: Can be purchased at the market packed in metal containers or waxed cartons in pint or quart sizes. They are usually sold in various sizes: extra large (extra select or large selects); medium—standard or small; very small. The meat should be plump and a creamy color, and the liquid in which it is packed must be clear and free from pieces of shell. Oysters must be kept refrigerated and will keep from 7 to 10 days. Frozen, shucked oysters are available year round. Once thawed, they must never be refrozen.

Canned oysters: On the Atlantic and Gulf coasts canned oysters are available in cans of 7½ ounces (drained weight). Pacific Coast oysters are sold in cans of 5 to 8 ounces (drained weight).

OPENING AND SHUCKING OYSTERS

Oysters do not have to be opened if they are cooked whole. Just clean them. Your fish dealer will open oysters at the market and pack them on ice, but charge more for opening. However, if you want to do it yourself, here is the procedure to follow:

1. Scrub the shell clean with a stiff brush under cold running water.
2. (Optional) To help make it easier to open, the thin end (bill) can be broken off with a hammer.
3. Place the oyster flat on the table with the hinge toward the hand.
4. With the other hand, force a shucking knife between the shells opposite the hinged edge.
5. Cut the large abductor muscle attached to the flat upper shell, removing the shell with a quick motion.
6. Cut the lower end of the same muscle attached to the deep half of the shell. Remove any chips of shell that cling to the meat.
7. Either serve on the half-shell or remove the oyster from the shell and place it in a container.

A mechanical oyster shucker can be purchased in most appliance stores.

COOKING

Oysters in the shell can be baked, boiled, broiled, steamed, or used in a bouillabaisse or stew, or in any way you might like to see an oyster in the shell.

Shucked oysters are delicious in bisques, chowders, soups, stews, fritters, patties, pies, or baked, broiled, deep-fat fried, pan fried, creamed, stuffed in poultry, or raw as a cocktail.

Don't let the oysters become shriveled while cooking or they will be tough. Cook only enough to heat them through. They should never lose their plumpness.

Approximate Amounts per Serving:

Oysters on the half-shell:
    6 large, 12 medium, 36 to 48 tiny
Shucked:
    ½ pint

Canned:

2 No. 1 cans serve 6 people

- Use plenty of lemon when serving oysters. Lemon counteracts the high acid-ash reaction that can result in an acid stomach.
- Oysters are excellent served with a starch, like potato salad, and cole slaw

- Serve raw oysters very cold on the half-shell. Place them on a bed of cracked ice and serve as the accompaniments: caviar, cocktail sauce, lemon wedges, or fresh pepper. Serve with rye or pumpernickel bread and plenty of butter.

BAKED OYSTERS

24 oysters
2 tablespoons caviar
2 tablespoons butter
2 tablespoons flour
Half the oyster liquid

½ cup fish stock or bottled clam juice
½ egg yolk
1½ tablespoons chives, minced
½ teaspoon fresh lemon juice
Salt and pepper to taste

Steam open oysters, saving the liquid, and keep them on one half of the shell. Put a small amount of caviar on each oyster. Preheat oven at 450°F. Melt butter in a saucepan over very low heat. Add flour and cook for 2 minutes. Gradually add oyster

liquid and fish stock until sauce is smooth and thickened. Combine all ingredients and simmer for 5 minutes. Put 1 teaspoon of sauce on each oyster. Bake in oven for 5 minutes.

FRIED OYSTERS

Drain oysters from their liquid. Dry them with paper towels. Sprinkle lightly with salt and pepper. First dip into flour, then bread crumbs, then egg beaten with water (1 egg

with 1 tablespoon water), and again into bread crumbs. Deep fry. (See Deep-Fat Frying, Chapter 12).

OYSTERS WITH BACON

24 oysters
12 strips bacon, halved crosswise

Salt and pepper to taste
Dash paprika

Drain oysters and pat dry with paper towels. Place each oyster on each piece of bacon. Sprinkle lightly with salt, pepper, and paprika. Wrap bacon around oyster and secure with a toothpick. Place oysters on a broiler pan.

Broil 3 inches from the flame for 3 minutes on each side or until bacon is crisp. Remove toothpick. Serve oysters with toast triangles or prepared toast squares.

OYSTERS ROCKEFELLER

---

18 shucked oysters, drained (save shells)
1 cup spinach, cooked
2 tablespoons onion, chopped
2 sprigs fresh parsley
1 bay leaf

¼ teaspoon celery salt
¼ teaspoon salt
3 drops Tabasco sauce
¼ cup dry bread crumbs
Lemon slices

Preheat oven to 400°F. Place oysters in deeper half of shells and place in a baking pan. Blend in a food grinder or processor onion, spinach, bay leaf, and parsley. Add remaining ingredients, except lemon and oysters. Blend well. Divide mixture on to oysters. Bake in oven for 10 minutes. Garnish with lemon slices. Serves 2 to 3.

POACHED OYSTERS FLORENTINE

(See Poaching, Chapter 15.) In scallop shells, place a layer of cooked spinach, to which a small amount of butter has been added.

Place poached oysters on top of the spinach. Cover with Mornay Sauce (see Chapter 17) and sprinkle with grated Cheddar, or Parmesan cheese. Place under broiler until cheese is melted and begins to turn brown.

Perch

FRESHWATER (blue pike perch, yellow pike perch, sauger, walleye)
OCEAN (red perch, redfish, rosefish, sea perch)

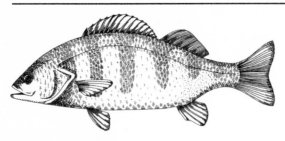

Perch is the common name for members of the family *Percedae*. The perch is related to the sunfish and the sea bass and is found both in the ocean and in shallow fresh water. It is among the most highly developed fish, dating back more than 100 million years.

Perch is a small and often brilliantly colored fish, although the most common perch is dark olive with brass-colored mottling and a pink stomach. Faint oblique bars cover the body which is slender with spiny fins. If not handled properly, the spikes on the forward dorsal fin can inflict a painful sting.

Perch travel in large schools and feed on insects, crustaceans, and smaller fish.

FRESHWATER PERCH

Pike perches, the largest variety, are the only freshwater species and all belong to the yellow-perch family. They include blue pike perch with spotless, slate blue bodies, weighing up to 2 pounds; yellow pike perch with yellowish, blotchy sides and a dark spot at the rear of the dorsal fin, weighing 3 to 7 pounds; sauger with 2 or 3 rows of round, black spots and a yellow caudal fin, weighing 1 to 2 pounds; and walleye, with small canine teeth, and bodies mottled with a black spot at the end of the spiny dorsal fin, weighing 1 to 4 pounds.

Yellow perch, often called red perch, is considered the best flavored of all freshwater fishes. When young, they are silver, but, as they mature the back turns a greenish gold with bright yellow sides (the color varies in intensity), and a white stomach. About 6 to 9 dark stripes run vertically across the body. The fins are usually a red or orange with a black spot on the spiny dorsal fin. They weigh ½ to 1 pound. All freshwater perch have firm, lean, white meat and a luscious, sweet, mild flavor.

OCEAN PERCH

Ocean perch is a term applied to the frozen fillets of the following marine fish: rosefish, redfish, red perch, and sea perch. The fillets of these fish are easily recognized by the flesh which is spotted with either pink or reddish coloring. The flesh is firm and coarse, and when cooked is white, flaky and extremely delicate in flavor. Some people think ocean perch is rather bland, which makes it ideal for those who like the texture of fish, but don't like fishy flavors. Ocean perch is easy to prepare and an attractive food to serve.

LOCATION

Freshwater perch are native to shallow

waters all over the northeastern United States from the Great Lakes to the upper Mississippi Valley, and from the Hudson Bay drainage to North Carolina. Perch have been transplanted into western waters in Washington, California, and the Ohio Valley. Ocean perch are found off the Atlantic Coast from Cape Cod to eastern Nova Scotia.

MARKET

Freshwater perch is available all year and are easily obtainable, especially in the Midwest. They are marketed whole, filleted, and frozen. Ocean perch is sold only frozen in fillets with or without the skin. They are packaged about six fillets to a pound and rarely have any bones.

COOKING

Small freshwater perch are especially good pan fried. Large sizes can be filleted for broiling or deep-fat frying, or used in chowders. Because ocean perch is bland, it can be cooked in many ways: frying, baking, broiling, or steaming. This fish is excellent with sauces and all combinations of foods.

Fillets have to be thawed overnight in the refrigerator (see Thawing Frozen Fish, Chapter 2), if they are to be breaded or stuffed. They can be cooked frozen, but you should allow additional cooking time.

- Stuff small perch with orange rice stuffing (see Chapter 21) and bake.

Pike

MUSKELLUNGE
PICKEREL

Pike is a common name for a small group (five species in North America) of freshwater fish of the family *Esocidae*, that include muskellunge; pike; and three species of pickerel called jack pike, jackes (Canadian), lake pickerel, lake pike, or northern pike.

The pike is long and thin with a spineless dorsal fin and large anal fin. Both fins are placed far back on the body, giving it a powerful tail. It has yellow eyes and a huge, long head. The jaw is long and narrow and the large mouth is studded with powerful needle-sharp teeth as well as small teeth on the tongue. Although it sheds its teeth, no great number is lost at one time so its ferocious eating habits are not hindered. The pike is carnivorous and cannibalistic, consuming one-fifth of its weight daily in fish, frogs, snakes, and young aquatic waterfowl and mammals, devouring them whole and instantly. The pike is a fierce fighter and capable of ingesting fish its own size.

The most common pike is greenish brown, usually with small, elongated white or yellow spots, arranged in rows on the head and body, with dark, oblong or round markings on the tail and fins; some pike are pale, others are dark silver with no spots. Each scale on the body has a gray V-shaped marking. The muskellunge is the largest fish in the pike family. It can weigh as much as 70 pounds and grow up to 5 feet long, but the average is 6 to 15 pounds. It is easily identified by the scaleless lower half of the cheek and gill cover. The muskellunge is usually dark gray with a round, or square, black spot on the side. All pike have lean flesh. Pike average 1½ to 10 pounds.

LOCATION
Pike enjoy quiet waters in the Great Lakes and surrounding states, the lakes of Canada, the St. Lawrence River, the waters from New York to the mouth of the Ohio River, or the Tennessee River. They are found in the Pacific from Alaska to the Arctic Circle.

MARKET
Pike are in season all year. Small fish are marketed whole; large fish are sold as fillets both fresh and frozen.

COOKING
Pike are more tender when purchased small.

Large pike tend to be dry when cooked because of their leanness and should always be braised. Pike have very small scales that are not easily removed. Some people leave them on. It is preferable to skin the whole fish after cooking or fillets or pieces before cooking to avoid eating the scales. If small enough, fish can be pan fried. Whole fish can also be stuffed and baked or broiled. Baste frequently with plenty of oil and butter. Fillets and chunks can be fried, deep-fat fried, and broiled. Whole fish and fillets are excellent poached or steamed in any court bouillon and served with a Hollandaise sauce, Béarnaise sauce, shrimp sauce, anchovy butter, or lemon butter.

- Cold pike is one of the most delicate and flavorful of white fish. Serve with a verte sauce, remoulade sauce, or olive oil mayonnaise.
- Because pickerel is bony, the following method of cooking is best: Fillet the pickerel and leave the skin on. (Because the scales are very small, scaling is not necessary.) Lay the skin side down on the cutting surface and slash the meat with a sharp knife. The slashes should be close together and extend from one end of the fillet to the other. *Do not cut through the skin.* Then cut the fillet into small pieces and deep fry them (See Deep-fat Frying, Chapter 12). The bones can be eaten along with the meat.

PIKE PARMESAN

3 pounds whole pike, cleaned	Cheddar, or Swiss
1 cup sour cream	½ teaspoon salt
4 tablespoons clarified butter (see Chapter 17)	¼ teaspoon pepper
½ cup grated cheese, Parmesan,	Watercress or other greens

Preheat oven to 350°F. Blend together sour cream, butter, cheese, salt, and pepper. Place pike in an oiled baking dish. Spread sour-cream mixture over entire fish. Bake for 30 minutes or until done (see Baking, Chapter 9). Garnish fish with greens. Serves 2.

BAKED PIKE

---

2 pike fillets, skinned and halved lengthwise
1 tablespoon onion, minced
¼ cup rice, uncooked
1 tablespoon clarified butter (see Chapter 17)

½ cup fish stock or bottled clam juice
1 teaspoon lemon juice
Salt and pepper
1½ ounces mushrooms, sliced lengthwise
Melted butter

Preheat oven to 350° F. In a saucepan, sauté onion and rice in butter until the onion has browned (approximately 5 to 7 minutes). Add fish stock, lemon juice, and salt and pepper. Bring to a boil, cover, reduce heat, and simmer until rice is cooked (approximately 20 minutes). Blend in mushrooms. Place fillets on an oiled baking pan. Divide rice mixture up evenly on the fillets. Roll the fillets around the mixture. Put ends on baking pan or secure with toothpicks, or poultry pins. Brush the top with butter. Bake approximately 25 to 30 minutes or until done. Baste often during cooking. Serves 2. Serve with the following sauce poured over cooked fish.

WHITE SAUCE

---

2 tablespoons butter
2 tablespoons flour
½ cup fish stock or bottled clam juice
½ cup milk

Almond slivers, toasted in a skillet without oil until browned.
Salt and pepper to taste

In a saucepan over low heat melt butter, add flour, and cook for 2 minutes. Gradually add liquid, stirring constantly until sauce is smooth and thickened. Season with salt and pepper to taste. Pour sauce over cooked pike and sprinkle with almonds. Serves 2.

Pompano

Pompano is a common name for the genus *Trachinotus* and *Palometus simillinus*. There are over 200 species of pompano.

The pompano is a plump fish with a compressed body and a blunt head. It has a horizontal mouth with teeth that appear during early development and disappear with age. The tail is deeply forked and the dorsal fin can be often seen above the surface of the water. The scales are very small and smooth, and the fish usually casts a silver or gold phosphorescence. The color varies from bright to dull. The palometa has a blue back with shiny yellow sides. It can weigh as much as 30 pounds and grow to a length of 3 feet, but the average weight is usually under 3 pounds. Pompano prefer warm seas, living on sandy bottoms and migrating when the season changes. An unseasonal cold spell will kill them. They feed on small crustaceans and bivalve mollusks, their favorite being shrimp and sand fleas. Pompano flesh is lean with a rich but delicate flavor.

California pompano, which are ex-tremely popular on the West Coast, are actually not members of this family but are closely related to the butterfish.

LOCATION
Pompano are found in warm seas around the world. In the United States, they are abundant in the South Atlantic from the Carolinas to the Gulf of Mexico.

MARKET
Pompano can be purchased year round but are most abundant from January to April. They are sold whole. The large ones can be filleted. Pompano is also available frozen. Florida pompano is available only locally or shipped north to better restaurants but never found in the market.

COOKING
Small, whole pompano are excellent pan fried and large fish can be baked. The fish can be served with Béarnaise sauce, anchovy butter, or Hollandaise sauce. Larger pompano can be filleted and cooked in any way.

- Broil and serve with lemon wedges, anchovy butter, or lemon butter.
- Pompano do not have to be scaled or skinned unless it is desired.

Porgy

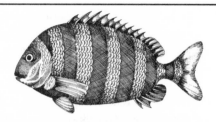

Porgy is a common name for members of the family *Sparidae* that contains 100 species, 24 of them in American waters. This family includes pagues, scup in New England, porgy in New York, fair maid in the South, red porgy or sea bream in Europe (a beautiful red fish with blue spots), and sheepshead (not related to the freshwater sheepshead of the croaker family), a porgy found mainly in the South.

The American porgy has an elongated body with 10 to 13 dorsal spines and 3 spines on a short anal fin. The mouth is small with strong canine and molar teeth designed for crushing food that consists of shellfish and other crustaceans. The dorsal color is brown tinted with pink and the stomach is silver. The average weight is ½ to 2 pounds, but 4-pound porgies are sometimes available and they have been known to reach 20 pounds. The sheepshead has two different colorings: broad black crossbars and yellow lengthwise stripes over faint crossbars.

Porgy flesh is tender, lean, flaky, and delicately flavored.

LOCATION
Porgies prefer warm and tropical waters such as the Mediterranean Sea, Red Sea, West Indies, Gulf of Mexico, and the coasts of Florida and California.

MARKET
The season is from January to November and the fish are marketed whole in weights under 2 pounds. Porgy is difficult to find inland but is bountiful in coastal markets. It is rarely available filleted.

COOKING
Because removing the scales is difficult, it is much easier to skin the fish. Do this after cooking with a whole fish and before cooking with fillets (see Skinning, Chapter 7).

- When small, they are excellent pan fried, served with tartar sauce.
- Large ones can be baked, served with a tangy sauce.
- If the porgy is large enough to fillet, pan fry and serve with any of the butters.

Salmon

BLUEBACK (Sockeye, Redfish)   **HUMPBACK (Pink Salmon)**
CHINOOK (King Salmon)   **SILVER OR COHO**
CHUM

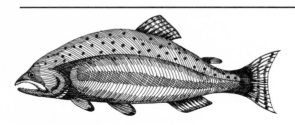

Salmon is a common name for members of the family *Salmonidae* that includes trout (see Trout). The North American species are valuable food fish, both fresh and canned. As marine fish, they spawn in fresh water and migrate to the sea where they inhabit cold, oxygen-rich waters at temperatures below 50°F. The distinctive characteristics of all salmon are their soft, rayless, adipose fins and their extremely good sense of smell.

In the sea, salmon are silver and live on crustaceans. In streams and rivers their coloring varies from black to bluish green on top with silver undersides marked with black spots. They feed mainly on smaller fish.

Salmon flesh is firm, fatty, flaky, and moist, except for the landlocked salmon which has very lean flesh. All have a sweet, rich flavor. The flesh varies in color from white to orange, pink, or red and is prized according to richness and brightness of color. Salmon generally weigh from 3 to 20 pounds.

The Atlantic salmon lives a complete life cycle in fresh water. It either avoids the sea or lives in landlocked bodies of water. The coloring is black to olive on the back with irregular black spots and silver sides. The male has red spots. Atlantic salmon weigh 2 to 4 pounds. The flesh is not as firm as the popular Pacific species which are commercially the most important.

The Pacific salmon has a long body and a wide mouth with teeth that become greatly enlarged during the breeding season. It is gray with blue or olive sides with a silver stomach. The head is darker than the body with very few spots, and the dorsal and caudal fins are black with round spots.

THE SALMON'S BASIC LIFE PATTERN

The first year or two is spent in fresh water. The salmon then voyages downstream into salt water where it matures, taking from 1 to 9 years. During the fall when it reaches prime condition, it stops eating and heads for spawning grounds. The Pacific salmon is famous for spectacular journeys of hundreds of miles, smelling its way back to the parent streams, traveling upstream over rapids, waterfalls, and through fast currents to reach the hatching sites inland. The chinook make the longest runs. Because the spawning salmon does not eat, the flesh becomes dry due to lack of oil. The journey is beset with the dangers of crowding, abrasive gravel, and fierce fights among male salmon. Those that survive the journey spawn and die. Both male and female die before the eggs hatch. The Atlantic salmon's journey is not as hazardous, and the fish may survive two or three spawnings.

The flesh of Pacific salmon is valued according to its depth of color—the deeper the better. The varieties of Pacific salmon (with the name given on the can) are:

BLUEBACK (sockeye, redfish): Red flesh, weighs from 3 to 10 pounds. During spawning, the male develops a pronounced hump on the back and the body grows slabsided. The blood-red head turns green and the snout grows long and very hooked. The blueback enjoys being landlocked. However, it could go back to the sea and survive.

CHINOOK (king salmon): Very pale pink to reddish flesh, weighing from 20 to 100 pounds. Chinook is the largest salmon. As it travels upstream to spawn, the gray-backed body turns black and blotched with dull orange-red. The tail turns cherry red and the jaws grotesquely hooked and savage-looking.

CHUM: During spawning, the male turns red and its nose becomes hooked. The chum has very light flesh.

HUMPBACK (pink salmon): Pink flesh; the smallest salmon, weighing 3 to 5 pounds. The humpback has many oblong spots on the caudal fin. The scales on the body are very small. The breeding male is red, blotched with brown tints and develops a bony hump on its back.

SILVER OR COHO: Usually distinguished by the spots on the top of its head. The flesh is medium red. The nose becomes hooked during spawning like that of other salmon. It can weigh from 3 to 15 pounds.

LOCATION

In the North Atlantic, salmon can be found from Maine to Labrador, Greenland and Europe, north of the Labrador coast, the Great Lakes, Nova Scotia, New Hampshire, Massachusetts, and Connecticut. Atlantic salmon make up very little of the commercial catch because of the excess slaughter that has made them scarce. In the Pacific, they can be found in the Columbia River, Puget Sound, Oregon, Alaska, and freshwater streams in which they spawn.

Canning centers are located on the Columbia River, Puget Sound, British Columbia, Siberia, and northern Japan. Alaska supplies canned salmon to over half the world.

MARKET

Because of the many forms of marketing, salmon is available year round. Fresh salmon is at a peak during the summer and fall and is marketed as steaks and fillets of the tail section. Canned salmon comes in various grades (see description of Pacific Coast salmon) and the quality is designated by different terms on the label. Salmon cheeks are a delicacy and are usually kippered and packed in glass jars or cans and used for appetizers. Fresh cheeks are the size of a half dollar and are very expensive. Salmon is available frozen in both steaks and fillets, and is also smoked, salted, and kippered.

COOKING

Salmon has very small scales and doesn't have to be scaled, unless desired. It is an oily fish and can be cooked in any way, served with or without sauces. Use mild sauces or one of the butters to enhance the delicious taste of salmon. Frozen salmon can be thawed and used in the same ways as fresh (see Thawing Frozen Fish, Chapter 2). Occasionally a small, whole salmon can be purchased. Fresh steaks or fillets can be baked or broiled. As a rule, salmon is better baked than broiled. Rub rosemary, dill, or tarragon on the fish, then brush with oil or butter or put the herbs in the melted butter.

- Poach salmon in a court bouillon and serve with a Hollandaise sauce, Béarnaise sauce, remoulade sauce, parsley sauce, or white sauce with egg.
- Cold poached salmon is delicious. Poach salmon in a highly spiced court bouillon. Chill and garnish with cucumbers, tomatoes, greens, and lemon wedges. Serve with mayonnaise, remoulade sauce, vinaigrette, tartar sauce or verte sauce.
- Fresh salmon cheeks should be flavored lightly and pan fried in a mixture of half butter and half oil. Serve with lemon wedges.
- Salmon roe can be sautéed or poached.
- Kippered salmon is cooked while being smoked. Heat and serve or flake it and combine it lightly with horseradish, chopped dill and sour cream. This makes an excellent sandwich spread or serve on crackers or toast for canapes.
- Salted salmon, salmon belly, and salmon tips must be soaked in cold water for several hours or overnight in the refrigerator to reduce the saltiness. Afterward steam or poach until flaky; serve with a béchamel sauce and sprinkle chopped, hard-cooked egg on top. This can also be served on toast.
- Canned salmon is excellent in salads, sandwiches, and casseroles accompanying noodles or vegetables. Use all the canned salmon, the liquid, bones, and skin; they are rich in calcium, iodine, phosphorous, and vitamins A, B, and D. A 4-ounce can of salmon has 150 calories compared to 450 calories in 4 ounces of lamb chops.

A sprinkling of citrus juices—lime, lemon, or orange—adds to the flavor of any salmon dish.

SALMON WITH EGG SAUCE

Prepare salmon for poaching in salted water (see Poaching, Chapter 15).

Prepare Sauce with the following:
- 1 tablespoon butter
- 1 tablespoon flour
- 1 cup milk or ½ cup fish stock or bottled clam juice and ½ cup milk

- 1 teaspoon Worcestershire sauce
- 2 eggs, hard-cooked and chopped
- 1 teaspoon fresh parsley, chopped, or ½ teaspoon dried parsley flakes
- 2 tablespoons dry sherry
  Salt to taste (optional)

Melt butter in a saucepan over very low heat. Add flour and cook for 2 minutes. Gradually add milk or stock, stirring constantly until sauce is smooth and thickened.

Add remaining ingredients.
Poach salmon. Pour sauce over cooked salmon.

SMOKED SALMON

On individual plates place very thin slices of smoked salmon. Sprinkle a few capers and chopped, hard-cooked egg over each serving. Top with chopped sweet onion. Serve with bread and butter. Or serve with the following sauce.

SAUCE FOR SMOKED SALMON

¼ cup mustard, French or English style
¼ cup sweet, brown German mustard
2 teaspoons sugar
2 tablespoons oil

1 tablespoon vinegar, white, cider, or tarragon
Salt and pepper to taste
1 tablespoon fresh dill, minced

Combine mustards and blend in sugar. Add oil, a few drops at a time, beating constantly until thick and smooth. Gradually add enough vinegar to thin sauce slightly. Season with salt and pepper and more sugar or vinegar, if desired. Blend in dill right before serving. Pour over cooked salmon or serve on the side. Makes ½ cup.

PAPRIKA SALMON

4 steaks
Flour
Paprika
6 tablespoons clarified butter (see Chapter 17)

1½ cups sour cream
½ cup dry white wine
Salt to taste

Put some flour and paprika into a plastic bag (about ⅛ teaspoon paprika to every ¼ cup flour—more or less paprika depending on your taste). Place one steak at a time into plastic bag and shake gently, coating steaks thoroughly. Sauté steaks quickly in butter until cooked (see Sautéing, Chapter 12). Remove from pan and season with salt. Keep warm on a warming plate or in low heated oven. Prepare sauce.

SAUCE

Mix wine with pan juices and cook down to ¼ cup. Add sour cream. Heat but do not boil because boiling will thin the sour cream to a watery consistency. Season with salt if necessary. Pour over salmon. Steaks can be served with rice or toast.

SESAME SALMON

Marinate salmon in soy sauce for 2 hours (do not add salt; soy sauce is salty enough). Poach (see Poaching, Chapter 15). Stir a handful of sesame or poppy seeds in a dry, ungreased frying pan over low heat until toasted. Sprinkle over poached salmon before serving.

Sardines see Herring

Scallop (or Pecten)

The Scallop is a marine bivalve mollusk with fan-shaped, beautifully scalloped shells. At the hinge, where the two valves meet, are flared ears or wings with radiating ribs. The scallop has no siphons. The mantle is open, and unlike other mollusks, both mantle edges have a row of steel-blue eyes and tactile projections.

The scallop moves around in the water in leaps and bounds by snapping its shell, which is controlled by a strong abductor muscle. This is the part of the scallop that frequently is eaten, although the whole scallop is edible. Europeans eat the whole scallop, and no one seems to know why Americans eat only the muscle.

The tiny bay scallop, 2 inches long, is extremely tender and more succulent than the larger, sea scallop, and is so popular that the supply has greatly diminished. The sea scallop grows to 5 inches with the muscle 1½ inches thick and 1½ inches long. The sea scallop is the more abundant of the two.

The meat of the scallop is white and firm. Bay and sea scallops are equally delicious if prepared with a light hand. Scallops are high in protein, containing little or no fat.

LOCATION
Bay scallops are found in shallow offshore waters and mudflats from Cape Cod to

Texas and inshore waters around Long Island. Giant sea scallops are found offshore in deep waters from Labrador to New Jersey.

MARKET

Scallops are harvested from September to April but are marketed year round. They are shucked, iced, and packed at sea and marketed both fresh and frozen. Fresh scallops are available only locally and rarely found fresh inland or on the West Coast. More common is the breaded, frozen, and ready to cook form. One pound serves 2. Bay scallops come 40 to a pound; sea scallops 18 to a pound.

COOKING

Broil, fry, or sauté; use in chowders, soups, or stews.

To broil scallops
1. Preheat broiler.
2. Place the scallops on a baking pan or broiler pan.
3. Brush with a mixture of half butter and half vegetable oil (optional: crushed garlic) and sprinkle lightly with salt and white pepper.
4. Place the pan 3 inches from the flame.
5. Scallops cook and turn brown in 5 to 6 minutes; do not overcook.
6. Place on a serving dish, pour the juices from the broiler pan on the scallops and serve with lemon wedges.

GARLIC SCALLOPS

This recipe can be prepared ahead of time and refrigerated until ready to cook.

1 pound scallops
3 cloves garlic, crushed
2 tablespoons clarified butter (see Chapter 17)

2 tablespoons fresh parsley, chopped, or 1 tablespoon dried parsley flakes
2 tablespoons scallions, minced
½ teaspoon dried tarragon
¼ teaspoon pepper
½ teaspoon salt

Wash scallops and dry thoroughly with paper towels. Sauté garlic in butter until brown, and remove garlic. Add remaining ingredients except scallops and cook for 2 minutes. Put scallops into a shallow baking pan. Pour butter mixture over scallops. Refrigerate, if desired, at this point. When ready to cook, broil in a preheated broiler for 4 minutes on each side or until brown. Baste during cooking. Serves 2.

SAUTÉED SCALLOPS

1 pound bay scallops
1 clove garlic, crushed
2 tablespoons clarified butter (see Chapter 17)

Paprika
1 tablespoon fresh parsley, chopped
2 tablespoons lemon juice
Salt and pepper to taste

Wash scallops and dry thoroughly with paper towels. Sauté garlic for 1 minute in butter and remove garlic. Add scallops and sauté until golden brown in color. Add remaining ingredients. Serves 2.

Shark

Sharks are mostly predatory fish of more than 250 species, ranging in size from the 2-foot pygmy shark to 50-foot giants. Sharks have no bones. The body consists of large deposits on a cartilage structure. The skin is leathery, covered with tiny, toothlike denticles. The nose is pointed with the mouth set on the lower part of the body. The teeth are triangular and are set in several rows. Shark gills are unprotected by any covering and, in most species, are set in rows of five on both sides of its body. In some species there are two more gill openings on the head called *spiracles*. Like bony fishes, sharks breathe by passing water through the mouth and over the gills which absorb the oxygen in the water. They must continuously move in order to breathe and to stay afloat and alive.

Sharks are excellent swimmers, propelling themselves swiftly with their sweeping tails. The upward curvature of the tail and the wide pectoral fins provide the lift as they move.

Most species bear their young live. The smaller sharks lay eggs encased in a horny shell containing a large quantity of yolk.

The shark's intestine has a spiral valve that increases the area of absorption. They are scavengers and gluttonous eaters, always killing more than they can devour.

There are a few harmless species that feed only on plankton. Only some predatory species attack humans unprovoked. Among these are the great white whale (maneater); the mako shark, (dark blue with a pure white belly and narrow, smooth teeth), the tiger shark, and the blue shark. These sharks are extremely sensitive to motion and the scent of blood.

Most shark meat is edible and nutritious with a mild flavor. It is coarse-textured but appetizing, especially the brown, dusky, hammerhead, leopard, and mako sharks and the soupfin. Others have a strong disagreeable taste. Sharks are used commercially mainly for Vitamin A, which is obtained from the liver. The flesh is used for poultry feed; the skin to make sandpaper (shagreen) as well as a durable leather for wallets, belts, and shoes.

LOCATION
Sharks are found in all seas, especially warmer waters and some large rivers. Shark fisheries are located on the Pacific Coast and on the coast of North Carolina and Florida.

MARKET
The season for shark is year round. Sharks are large and are prepared as steaks, fillets, and chunks, both fresh and frozen.

COOKING
Shark can be cooked in anyway desired. As steaks, it has a texture and flavor similar to swordfish. Soupfin is excellent when kippered. Cantonese chefs use the calcium-rich fins to make a delicious and complicated gelatinous soup.

SHARK STEAK

1 steak per person Marinate steaks for 24 hours in a mixture of the following ingredients: ½ cup lemon or lime juice 2 tablespoons prepared horseradish ½ tablespoon salt	¼ teaspoon pepper ½ cup oil 1 tablespoon grated lemon, lime, or orange rind ½ teaspoon dried basil or 1 teaspoon fresh basil ½ teaspoon dried oregano

After marinating, place steaks in a shallow baking pan and broil 6 inches from flame for 7 minutes on each side. Baste steaks frequently with marinade.

Shad see Herring

Shrimp and Prawns

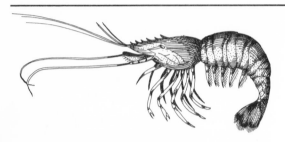

Shrimp and prawns are small crustaceans with 10 jointed legs attached to the thorax and swimmerets attached to the abdominal segments. The body is compressed laterally, and the thin, smooth, almost transparent exoskeleton is shed periodically as the shrimp or prawn matures. The term prawn is applied loosely to large shrimp, but a true prawn has a strong body and tail, a toothed beak (rostrums) with a prominent grooved head, long antennae, and slender legs. Shrimp and prawns can grow to a length of 9 inches but are usually found much smaller. Tiny brine shrimp that are smaller than 1 inch belong to a completely different subclass of crustacean and are not a true shrimp. Shrimp swim, rather than crawl, unlike their relatives, the lobster and crab. They are also able to swim backward quickly with their paddlelike tails.

In American waters the shrimp is grayish green or greenish brown. A new species found on the Gulf Coast is pink. The brown shrimp found in markets is from Brazil. All shrimp and prawns turn pink and white when cooked and there is little or no differ-ence in flavor and texture. Both shrimp and prawns have lean flesh with a firm white texture. They are an excellent source of minerals—calcium, phosphorous, sulphur, and copper—and high in iodine and protein and low in calories. They have a few water-soluable vitamins.

A bizarre tropical species of shrimp, the pistol shrimp, has a large claw adapted from one of its appendages with a movable finger. When the claw is snapped closed, the sound waves kill or incapacitate nearby prey.

LOCATION
Shrimp and prawns are abundant in both fresh and salt waters in temperate and tropical conditions. Large commercial catches are made on the coasts of Virginia, Louisiana, and the Gulf of Mexico.

MARKET
Shrimp are available year round. The peak of the season for average sizes is August through December; for jumbo sizes, March through June.

Fresh shrimp should have a tight-fitting shell around the body. Any shrinkage of the flesh can be a sign of staleness. If there is the slightest smell of ammonia, the shrimp are not fresh. Shrimp and prawns are sold fresh and cooked, shelled or unshelled. Sometimes the shelled fresh or cooked shrimp are deveined, ready for cooking. They are also available packaged raw frozen;

precooked; processed after they are peeled and deveined for a better flavor and then frozen; precooked, processed, breaded, and frozen; or cooked in their own juices and packed either dry or in brine in 4½-to 5-ounce cans. Frozen, stuffed jumbo shrimp are also available. Approximate quantities:

Small: 40 to 50 per pound
Average: 16 per pound
Jumbo: 10 to 12 per pound

One serving:

6 large (cocktails)
10 small (cocktails)
¼ to ⅓ pound, cooked

COOKING

The tail of the shrimp and prawn are the only part eaten. The head and thorax are removed usually before shrimp reach the market. Occasionally they can be purchased with the head, which should be removed before cooking.

PREPARING RAW SHRIMP AND PRAWNS FOR COOKING

1. Wash the shrimp in the shells thoroughly under cold running water.
2. Remove the shells by pushing with your thumb and forefinger. They will come off easily. The fan-shaped tail can be left on if you are going to make scampi, grill, or barbecue, or simply want them for appearance.
3. Deveining before cooking is much easier. Use the point of a knife to slit the outside curvature of the body and remove the black vein under cold running water. Some people skip the deveining, but removing the vein enhances the appearance of most dishes. Of course, shrimp that are served cold and boiled in the shells, cannot be deveined.

4. You can butterfly shrimp at this stage by cutting through the flesh as you remove the vein so that the two halves nearly but not completely separate.

Some recipes call for broiling butterfly shrimp in the shell. Devein and slit the shrimp in the shell, or slice the shrimp in half lengthwise, leaving the shrimp intact at the tail end. The shrimp or prawn is now ready for cooking and can be baked, deep-fat fried, pan fried, sautéed, used in bisques, broths, chowders, fritters, gumbos, or soups.

- Do not precook shrimp if they are to be added to a sauce or they will be tough.
- Bouillon from shrimp can be made by boiling the shells, and a couple heads if available, in water.
- Frozen shrimp should be thawed before using.
- Canned shrimp are good for sandwiches, spreads, stuffings and salads. Canned or cooked shrimp can be used in all recipes except those calling for deep-fat batter frying, broiling, and barbecuing. In these cases, the shrimp must be raw.
- Purchased precooked shrimp are fine for serving as cocktails, in salads, or any recipe calling for precooked shrimp (bisques, bouillabaisse, fritters, or patties).

BOILING SHELLED OR UNSHELLED SHRIMP TO BE SERVED COLD AS APPETIZERS OR IN SALADS

1. Bring to a boil enough salted water to just cover shrimp, (approximately 1 quart of water and 2 teaspoons salt per pound). Thyme, bay leaf, peppercorns, and a bouquet garni give extra flavor.
2. Add the shrimp, cover, bring to a boil.

Immediately remove from heat and let stand 2 to 5 minutes—*no longer*—depending on the size, until they become firm and turn white. If overcooked they will be tough and shrink more than necessary.

3. Drain and chill.

BROILED MARINATED SHRIMP

---

  1 pound raw shrimp, shelled and deveined
½ cup prepared mustard, French or English style

¼ cup honey
  1 tablespoon lemon or lime juice
½ teaspoon salt

Wash shrimp and dry with paper towels. Combine all ingredients. and marinate shrimp in refrigerator for 3 hours. When ready to cook, drain and reserve sauce.

Place shrimp in a shallow broiler pan. Broil in a preheated broiler for 5 minutes on each side. Baste with marinade during cooking.

FRIED SHRIMP IN BEER BATTER

---

*1*½ pounds large, raw shrimp, shelled and deveined, tails left intact (butterfly, if desired)
    Vegetable oil

BATTER

1 cup flour
1 teaspoon baking powder
¼ teaspoon salt
    Dash pepper

1 egg, lightly beaten
1 cup stale beer

In a mixing bowl combine flour, baking powder, salt, and pepper. Add egg. Gradually add beer until mixture is well blended. If lumps form strain mixture or start over. Allow mixture to sit at room temperature for 1 hour.

(See Deep-fat Frying, Chapter 12). Heat oil. Dip each shrimp into batter, then into oil. Cook approximately 5 minutes until golden brown. Do not overcook.

SHRIMP MEUNIÈRE

1 pound raw shrimp, shelled and
   deveined
3 tablespoons clarified butter (*see*
   Chapter 17)

1 tablespoon lemon or lime juice
½ teaspoon salt
⅛ teaspoon pepper

Wash shrimp and dry with paper towels.
Cook shrimp in butter for 5 to 10 minutes.
Be careful not to burn or overcook shrimp.

Remove shrimp to a hot plate. Add lemon
juice, salt, and pepper to pan juices. Heat
and pour over cooked shrimp.

SHRIMP SCAMPI

1 pound raw, large shrimp, shelled
   and deveined
2 tablespoons celery, minced
1 tablespoon onion, minced
1 teaspoon green pepper, minced
⅓ cup half oil and half clarified butter
   (see Chapter 17)
1 clove garlic, minced

1 tablespoon fresh parsley, chopped,
   or 1½ teaspoon dried parsley
   flakes
⅓ cup water
2 tablespoons lemon juice
⅓ cup tomato paste
½ teaspoon salt

Wash shrimp and dry with paper towels.
Sauté celery, onion, and pepper in oil-butter
combination until tender, approximately 4
minutes. Add remaining ingredients. Simmer
no more than five minutes more until
shrimp is done. Do not overcook or shrimp
will be tough.

Smelt

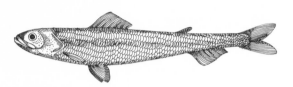

Smelt is the common name for the family *Osmeridae.* It is closely related to the salmon and has an outstanding flavor. Most species are found in salt water, but some run to fresh water to spawn in April. Smelts swarm by the millions during their spawning runs which can last for a week or more. Other species are landlocked in lakes. Smelts feed mostly on shrimp and other small crustaceans and are destructive and cannibalistic feeders.

Smelts have small, slender bodies, large heads, large eyes, soft fin rays, an adipose fin, and a tooth-lined tongue. Their coloring is grayish silver or olive on the back with bright silver sides, white belly, and dark-edged dorsal and caudal fins. Black and silver lines run lengthwise on the body.

The American smelt or icefish, the most important, can weigh up to 1 pound and grow as large 10 inches in length. The candlefish in the Northwest is so fatty, that when dried and furnished with a wick, it can burn as a candle. Both are outstanding for their extreme oiliness and succulence.

The flesh of most species is lean, very sweet, and delicately flavored. The Pacific smelt has an excellent flavor, but its flesh is soft and doesn't keep well. Other species have a tendency to absorb unpleasant flavors from the rivers in which they live and are inedible or extremely strong-flavored.

LOCATION
Smelts can be found in the Great Lakes, Michigan, New England, Oregon, San Francisco, Alaska, Northeast Asia, and in many lakes all over the world.

MARKET
The peak of the season is September to May. Runs begin as early as March and as late as the end of April. The average market size is 7 inches, but many are smaller. It can take as many as 11 smelt to make 1 pound. Smelt are marketed whole, either fresh or frozen.

COOKING
Smelt bones can be eaten if the smelt are tiny. Larger ones have tougher bones.

- Deep-fat fry or pan fry and serve with a tomato sauce.
- Broil or sauté and serve with tartar sauce or remoulade sauce.
- Marinate in lemon or lime juice for 1 hour, sauté, and serve with lemon or lime butter.
- Serve smelt with parsley deep fried for 2 minutes or until crisp.

BAKED SMELTS

1 pound smelts, cleaned
1 large onion, chopped
3 stalks celery, chopped
1 cup dry white wine
  Salt and pepper to taste

2 tablespoons butter, melted
  Grated cheese, Parmesan, Cheddar,
    or Gruyère

Preheat oven to 375°F. Dry smelts with paper towels. Place onion and celery at bottom of an oiled, shallow baking pan. Place smelts on top of vegetables. Pour wine over fish, season with salt and pepper, brush with melted butter. Bake in oven for 15 minutes (see Baking, Chapter 9). Remove from oven, sprinkle with cheese, and broil again until cheese turns brown.

FRIED SMELTS

1 pound smelts, cleaned
  Salt and pepper to taste
1 cup flour
¼ cup grated cheese, Parmesan
1 can (8 ounces) tomato sauce

Lemon juice
Cocktail sauce or tartar sauce
Lemon wedges
Vegetable oil

Dry smelts thoroughly with paper towels. Season inside of fish with salt and pepper. Combine flour and cheese in a plastic bag. Dip fish in tomato sauce seasoned with lemon juice. Place smelts into plastic bag, two at a time, and shake gently to coat. Deep fry, a few at a time, taking care not to crowd fish. (See Deep-fat Frying, Chapter 12). They cook in approximately 4 minutes. Drain cooked fish on paper towels. Serve with lemon wedges and cocktail sauce.

Snail

Snail is a common name for the gastropod—a mollusk with a muscular foot and a shell consisting of one valve. The snail has a single extremely well developed spiral shell into which it can withdraw in case of danger. The eyes are located on the ends of stalks or tentacles.

There are thousands of species, ranging from the American that is 1½ inches in diameter to the tropical species that is 6 inches and weighs 1 pound. Snails are found in fresh and salt water and also on land. The aquatic species, the periwinkle, breathes through gills. The land snail breathes from a pulmonary sac, or lung, in the mantle cavity. A few water species have lungs and rise to the surface for oxygen. The land snail is hermaphroditic but the majority of the aquatic species have separate sexes. The terrestrial species moves by rhythmic contractions of the muscular foot, leaving a slimy path. It causes great economic loss because it destroys vegetation. Snails served as *escargots* are land snails. Some species eat both vegetation and animal mat-

ter and others eat one or the other. American consumption of snails is increasing, but at present snails are not abundant fresh. Perhaps one reason Americans find them unappetizing is that some freshwater species harbor disease-carrying parasites.

LOCATION
Extremely abundant in France, Switzerland, and Italy, snails are also bountiful in Japan.

MARKET
The season for fresh snails is November to March. In the United States, fresh snails are seldom marketed and are rarely more than 1½ inches in diameter. Snails can be purchased canned, ready for cooking, with the shells canned separately. The shells can be reused many times before they wear out. Buy ¼ to ½ pound per person.

COOKING
Boil or steam live snails in their shells and use them in a bouillabaisse or broth. Broil or sauté.

To boil:
1. Clean snail shells with a stiff brush.
2. Remove the chalky partition that closes them.
3. Soak them overnight in enough cold water to cover them. Add a little salt.

4. The next day, wash them well again in cold running water, removing all the slime.

5. Put the snails in a saucepan; cover them with water. Boil them for 8 minutes.

6. Drain and rinse with cold water.

7. Put them back into the pan. Add white wine to cover, salt, pepper, large bouquet garni, onion stuck with 4 cloves, a couple of crushed garlic cloves, and brandy. Simmer for 3 hours. If snails are very large cook longer.

8. Remove from heat and allow to cool in cooking liquid.

9. Drain.

10. Remove from shell with special utensils for snail removal which can be purchased in gourmet stores. Remove the black end from each snail.

11. Wash the shells.

12. Stuff the snails back into the shell and fill with snail butter.

13. Arrange on a baking dish and bake for a few minutes until very hot.

SNAIL BUTTER

¼ pound butter
1 clove garlic, minced
3 shallots, minced

1 teaspoon parsley
Salt and pepper to taste

Blend all ingredients well, and stuff snails. Mix canned or cooked snails, whole or chopped, with garlic and butter, herbs, or pieces of anchovies. Place back in the shell and broil, brushing with more garlic and butter.

Stuff mushroom caps with chopped cooked or canned snails and broil or bake with garlic and butter.

Snapper

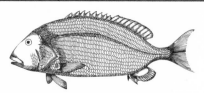

Snapper is the common name for members of the family *Lutianidae,* of which the most popular are the red, gray, and schoolmaster, or muttonfish, snapper. Snapper is found mainly in tropical coastal waters. The snapper has a large mouth with sharp jaw teeth. The top of the snout is flattened and the fins are spiny. The coloring is usually iridescent blue, yellow, and green with shades of red. The gray snapper has a dark olive head and bluish black dorsal fin. The tail fin is violet, the anal fin dark pink. The red snapper is deep red with a pale rose throat. The fins are red-edged with orange and black. Bluish streaks stretch across the scales. The snapper is a carnivorous and voracious feeder, traveling in dense schools. The size ranges from ½ pound for the gray snapper to 35 pounds and a length of 3 feet for the red snapper.

The meat of most snappers is tender, lean white with a delicate flavor, and it keeps extremely well. The red snapper is a fatty fish with a delicious, strong flavor.

LOCATION
Snappers are found in warm seas north of Long Island to the coast of Florida and Key West to the Gulf of Mexico.

MARKET
The season for snapper is year round. They are sold whole fresh in weights of ½ to 5 pounds. Larger fish are marketed in fillets and steaks, both fresh and frozen.

COOKING
Small snapper weighing 1½ pounds or less are excellent pan fried or baked. Prepare one fish per person. Large snappers can be boiled, broiled, steamed. Snapper baked with a stuffing is delicious. Fillets, steaks, and chunks can be cooked in any way.

- Snapper is excellent poached in a mild court bouillon, usually salt and water, and served with Béarnaise sauce.
- Cold, poached snapper can be served with sauce verte.
- After broiling fillets, sprinkle with toasted coconut. Serve with lemon or lime wedges.

BAKED GRAY SNAPPER

3 pounds snapper, whole	¼ teaspoon salt
¼ cup lemon or lime juice	⅛ teaspoon pepper, freshly ground

Combine juice with salt and pepper. Put fish into a dish and baste inside and out with juice. Cover and set aside in refrigerator to marinate until the following procedure is completed.

While fish is marinating prepare:
- ⅛ cup oil combined with ⅛ cup clarified butter (see Chapter 17)
- 1 large onion, thinly sliced
- ¼ teaspoon dried thyme leaves
- ¼ teaspoon oregano
- ⅛ teaspoon bay leaf crumbled
  Salt and pepper to taste

Pour 3 tablespoons oil-butter combination in bottom of a baking pan large enough to hold fish, place onion and herbs on top. Sprinkle with salt and pepper.

In a separate pan:
- 1 small onion, minced
- 1 small hot pepper, seeded and minced
- ½ teaspoon fresh parsley, chopped
- ¼ cup almonds toasted and ground (Sauté the nuts in an ungreased frying pan until brown, stirring constantly. Grind either in a blender or with a mortar and pestle).
- ¾ cup fish stock or bottled clam juice

Preheat oven to 350°F. Sauté the onion in the remaining oil-butter mixture until tender, about 5 minutes. Add the hot pepper, parsley, almonds and half the fish stock, blend well.

Put fish on top of onions in the baking pan. Place the almond mixture on top and along sides of the fish. Bake (see Baking, Chapter 9).

FRIED SNAPPER

- 2 fillets
- 1 medium onion, chopped
- 2 teaspoons fresh parsley, chopped, or 1 teaspoon dried parsley flakes
- Juice of 1 lemon
- ½ cup dry white wine
  Salt and pepper to taste

Put fillets into a frying pan. Cover with onions. Add remaining ingredients. Bring to a boil, cover, reduce heat, and simmer until tender (approximately 15 minutes). Serves 2.

Sole see Flatfish

Squid

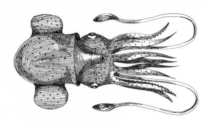

Squid—also called inkfish or cuttlefish—is a carnivorous marine cephalopod mollusk closely related to the octopus. The squid is a highly developed invertebrate. It has no shell but, instead, under the mantle (covering) is a horny plate shaped like a quill pen that provides interior support. The mantle is the main swimming apparatus and is shaped into lengthwise fins along the posterior the body, protruding like a collar around the head. The mantle contracts and relaxes, expelling water in a rapid series of jets from the muscular funnel located below the head and propelling the squid in any direction in quick, jerky movements.

The ten sucker-bearing arms help the squid move in a chosen direction. Two of these tentacles seize the prey and the squid's jaws cuts it into pieces. When the squid is in danger it emits a cloud of dark substance from its ink sac.

The squid breathes through gills and has a highly developed nervous system. In some species the organs are luminescent. The eyes are very similar to a human's—a case of convergent evolution with no common ancestor. Squid range in size from 2 inches to 50 feet. The meat is sweet and rich. Squid use to be a poor man's food but is now on the menus of luxury restaurants.

LOCATION
They are most abundant in the Atlantic Ocean from Labrador to the Carolinas and are often seen traveling in schools.

MARKET
The season is year round. They are marketed fresh, averaging about 1 foot long.

COOKING
For most preparations, the belly should be cut open with a knife and the cartilage pulled or cut out.

- Broil with butter and rosemary.
- Broil with a tart sauce or wine sauce.
- Cut tentacles into small pieces, flour the pieces, then coat with an egg-and-breadcrumb mixture or a batter and fry (see Frying, Chapter 12). Serve with tartar sauce or mustard sauce.
- Cut tentacles into small pieces, flour the pieces, and sauté (see Sautéing, Chapter 12). Cover pan to prevent splattering. Salt and pepper the squid and serve with puréed spinach seasoned with a small amount of garlic juice.

BAKED SQUID

Clean squid and marinate in milk for at least 1 hour. Roll squid in bread crumbs moistened with butter. Place squid on an oiled baking pan. Season with salt and pepper.

Dot with pieces of butter. Bake in a preheated 500°F oven for approximately 12 minutes. Serve with tartar sauce or tomato sauce.

Sturgeon

The sturgeon is a member of the family *Acipenseridae*. There are seven species of sturgeon in North American waters. The sturgeon is a beautiful and primitive fish, and possesses adaptive features of a high survival value.

Unlike other fish the sturgeon has fine-grained skin with very few scales. Instead, it has five to seven widely spaced rows of bony humps, or shields, extending lengthwise along the back and sides of the body. The tail fins are turned upward, with the dorsal fin located near the tail. The underslung mouth is set far back on the underside of the head. The mouth is toothless and fleshy. The sturgeon is one of the few fishes that have taste buds outside of the mouth.

It is an extremely slow eater, spending a great deal of time in search of food and eating. It feeds on crayfish, snails, and small fish by siphoning the food into the mouth. Its head tapers to a long, pointed, blunted or cone-shaped snout. The eyesight is poor so it relies on four barbels (whiskers) located below the nose to find food, moving like a mine detector over the bottom. The sturgeon varies in color from all white to brownish, gray brown or olive brown, with a pale or white belly.

Some sturgeon are marine fish, others ascend into rivers to spawn. Three species are strictly landlocked freshwater inhabitants and are the largest of all inland fish. Sturgeon can grow to a length of 13 feet and weigh as much as 1 ton. Their flesh is firm and meaty with a strong flavor. Many states prohibit fishing for sturgeon because of its scarcity. Sturgeon can take up to 20 years to mature. Artificial methods of propagation have failed with both freshwater and saltwater species.

LOCATION

In American waters, sturgeon are found only in the northern hemisphere. They can be found in the Great Lakes, Mississippi Valley, and Lake Huron. Smaller varieties are found in the Pacific. The largest species is the Russian beluga, found in the Caspian and Black Seas. The latter's eggs, or roe, are considered a delicacy (see Caviar).

MARKET

Fresh sturgeon is rarely seen in the markets. If you are lucky enough to find them fresh, lake sturgeon are superior in flavor to sea sturgeon. The season in the Columbia River fishery is from April to November. Smoked and kippered sturgeon is considered a delicacy. It is sold throughout the country all year and is very expensive. The roe of sturgeon is considered the best caviar.

COOKING

Fresh sturgeon flesh is firm and dry and needs frequent basting during cooking. The fish should be filleted, steaked or cut into chunks and skinned. They can be cooked in any way desired. Serve with lemon wedges or Béarnaise sauce.

- Coat the steaks with seasoned flour. (Put seasoned flour into a plastic bag, put the steaks into the bag one at a time and shake the bag gently until steaks are thoroughly covered with the flour.) Sauté (see Sautéing, Chapter 12). Serve with brown butter poured over cooked fish or with Béarnaise sauce, garnish with lemon wedges.
- Serve sliced smoked sturgeon with dark bread or in salads and casseroles.

Swordfish

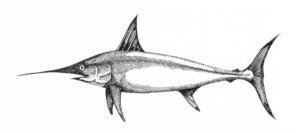

Swordfish belongs to the family *Xiphias gladius*. The characteristic that gives them their name is an oblong-shaped, upper jaw, sharp and broad, resembling a flattened sword. The swordfish has a long, sleek body, a long dorsal fin and two ventral fins. The adult has no teeth. The swordfish feeds on smaller fish, swimming beneath schools and attacking with their jaws and impaling their victims. It can grow to a length of 15 feet and weigh up to 1,000 pounds. Some species weigh as little as ½ pound. The flesh is firm, lean, and rich flavored.

Swordfish have a habit of lying just beneath the water's surface where their fins are mistaken for those of sharks. Captured by harpooning, they become vicious before they die and have been known to pierce the sides of boats with their jaws.

LOCATION

Swordfish are found in most warm coastal waters around the world: in Nova Scotia; from Cuba to Cape Breton; the South Pacific.

MARKET

A large quantity of swordfish is imported, making them available frozen year round.

The peak of the season for fresh swordfish in the Atlantic is April to September; in the Pacific from September to December. Swordfish is sold mainly in steak form, fresh or frozen, and is rarely found in any other form. Swordfish liver oil is rich in vitamins.

COOKING

Swordfish steaks are best broiled; they must be basted frequently during cooking or will become dry. Be careful not to overcook. Any sauce can be served with swordfish, but because of the great flavor, subtle sauces are best: lemon butter, tarragon butter, or lemon wedges.

SWORDFISH with barbecue sauce

2 Swordfish steaks	1½ teaspoons prepared mustard, French or English style
4 tablespoons butter	½ cup chili sauce
1 small onion, chopped	1 clove garlic, minced
1 tablespoon brown sugar	2 drops Tabasco sauce
1½ teaspoons Worcestershire sauce	

Preheat broiler. Combine all ingredients, except fish, in a saucepan and simmer for 20 minutes. Place fish on an oiled broiler pan. Sprinkle with salt and pepper. Baste with sauce. Broil 3 inches below flame (see Broiling, Chapter 10). Turn once, baste, and finish cooking. Serve with remaining sauce on the side. Serves 2.

BROILED SWORDFISH

2 swordfish steaks, ¾-inch thick	1 clove garlic, minced
2 tablespoons clarified butter (see Chapter 17)	1 teaspoon prepared mustard, French or English style
3 tablespoons lemon or lime juice	4 anchovy fillets, minced

Preheat broiler. Sauté garlic in butter for 2 minutes. Add lemon juice. Place steaks in a well-oiled broiling pan. Baste with half the lemon-garlic mixture just prepared. Broil 3 inches from flame. Broil for 7 minutes, then turn. Baste with mustard on other side. Sprinkle with anchovies and baste with lemon butter. Return to broiler and broil until done (approximately 5 minutes) and brown.

Trout

BLACK-SPOTTED TROUT (cutthroats)
BROOK TROUT (char, mountain trout, speckled trout)
GOLDEN TROUT
LAKE TROUT (mackinaw, togue)
RAINBOW TROUT (salmon trout)
SEA TROUT (gray sea trout, spotted sea trout, spotted weakfish, weakfish, white sea trout)

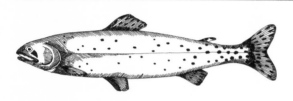

Trout is a member of the family *Salmonidae* that includes salmon (see Salmon in this Dictionary). Trout is a marine fish that spawns in fresh water, finding its way back to parent streams by smell. The trout thrives in cool waters below 60°F. The average weight is 3 pounds.

Some trout spawn more than once but the majority return to the sea. Landlocked species reproduce and live without any observable changes. However, there are as many variations in habits of the trout as there are species. All trout have fine scales. The eyes are large and the head is scaleless. The trout has a single dorsal and adipose fins, and a small, fleshy protuberance on the back between the dorsal and caudal fins. It is a beautiful fish. The size, color, and taste vary locally, depending on the abundance of food in the area and the temperature of the water. The colors range from very dark to bright with various designs: green-gray splotches with pale oval or bean-shaped spots. Well-fed trout are brightly colored with pinkish flesh; those living in a poorer

environment are more variegated. These variations in the meat are similar to the various grades of beef.

BLACK-SPOTTED TROUT (cutthroats)
When black-spotted trout return to the sea they are called *steelhead cutthroats*. The black-spotted trout is usually dark gray or olive gray with a silver stomach. There is a pair of large bright-red, horizontal streaks, or slash marks, underneath the throat. It is often heavily patterned with black spots of varying sizes and shapes, usually only on the head but sometimes extending over the stomach. Half-inch spots cover the dorsal, adipose, and caudal fins. Teeth grow only on the roof of the mouth. In the sea the black-spotted trout weighs up to 3 pounds. The freshwater variety can weigh up to 1 pound.

BROOK TROUT (char, mountain trout, speckled trout)
The brook trout is probably the most popular trout. It prefers the cold water in lakes and in streams that run in torrents. It has an elongated body, a large head, and a large mouth with a blunted snout. The scales of the trout are microscopic. The back is dark olive or black with intricate markings: dark blue or black bars or speckling. The sides

of the body are spotted with red markings, bordered with blue. The lower edge of the tail and lower fins are edged in white, orange, and deep orange. The belly of the male is usually red. Trout that run to the sea are silver in color. The brook trout averages less than 1 pound in small streams and grows to several pounds in larger bodies of water. The flesh is lean and mild flavored.

GOLDEN TROUT
The coloring of the golden trout is similar to the rainbow with brilliant orange and yellow markings. It rarely weighs more than 1 pound.

LAKE TROUT (mackinaw and togue)
A deep-water fish and the largest of the trout, it weighs up to 125 pounds. The usual weights range from 1½ to 10 pounds. The body is more elongated than that of other trouts, with a large flattened head, large mouth, and deeply forked tail. The coloring changes according to the season and temperature of the water. In the market, however, they are usually gray, pale green, dark green, and black, covered with irregular, light-yellow spots often tinged with pink. The top of the head is usually maroon. Lake trout flesh is pink or occasionally white and has a sweet, delicate, fatty flavor.

RAINBOW TROUT (salmon trout)
When the rainbow trout enters salt water it is called a steelhead. The rainbow trout has winding rows of teeth on the roof of the mouth. The back of the fish is olive or blue, the sides greenish bronze or silver with small dark spots covering most of the body. Their coloring is not necessarily of a rainbow hue; but, the brilliant reddish, pink, or light purple stripe extending the length of the fish is their identification mark. The stripe is brighter in the male. The rainbow trout can weigh as much as 40 pounds but averages 2 to 8.

SEA TROUT (gray sea trout, spotted sea trout, spotted weakfish, weakfish, and white sea trout)
The spotted sea trout is the most important food fish of the trout family. Sea trout weighs from 1 to 6 pounds, most averaging 2 pounds. The meat is white, lean, extremely tender (the reason they are called weakfish), and delicately flavored. Sea trout prefers warm waters but will occasionally venture into cool waters where its taste and texture is greatly affected. The white sea trout is the smallest with an exceptionally delicious flavor.

LOCATION

Black-spotted trout: Columbia River basin, Idaho, California, Alaska, Rocky Mountain states.

Brook trout: The Rockies, British Columbia, eastern North America, cold waters of California.

Golden trout: High Sierras at altitudes over 10,000 feet and cold waters of California.

Lake trout: The Greak Lakes, Maine, British Columbia, Alaska, North American lakes, Arctic Circle.

Rainbow trout: California, British Columbia, Alaska.

Sea trout: Atlantic Coast from Cape Cod to Texas. Spotted sea trout is found mainly from North Carolina to the Gulf of Mexico.

MARKET
Trout is available year round, but peaks in spring, summer, and fall. It is marketed

mainly as fresh and frozen whole fish. The larger species can be purchased as fillets. Trout is also available drawn and kippered, and as canned fillets.

COOKING

Small fish can be cooked any way, but are most popular pan fried and broiled with or without stuffing. The fillets of larger fish can be prepared in any way. The scales on some trout are very small and even embedded in the skin, making them difficult to remove. Skin either before or after cooking (see Skinning, Chapter 7). Brook trout does not have to be scaled, unless desired.

Poach trout in a water-and-vinegar bouillon. Trout takes only a few minutes to poach and care must be taken not to overcook. Serve with Béarnaise sauce, Hollandaise sauce, or shrimp sauce.

- After pan frying or sautéing, mix together in the pan ¼ cup chopped parsley, ¼ cup chopped tarragon, ½ cup dry white wine. Let sauce boil for 1 minute. Pour over the fish.
- Use a tangy sauce on rainbow trout.
- Charcoal-broil; serve with a spicy barbecue sauce.
- Smoked trout should be served with sweet cream and white horseradish.

POACHED TROUT

Oil or butter the bottom of a baking dish large enough to hold the fish. Scatter fennel on the bottom of the pan (about ¼ teaspoon per fish). Season the trout with salt and pepper. Place fish in pan. Pour enough white wine over the fish for poaching (see Poaching, Chapter 15). Poach. Remove cooked fish and keep warm. Reduce the liquid in the pan to half by boiling. Thicken the remaining liquid by adding small amounts of butter. Season if necessary. Pour over cooked fish.

SAUTÉED TROUT

Sauté whole fish in butter (see Sautéing, Chapter 12). Remove fish from pan after cooking.

Add 8 tablespoons clarified butter (see Chapter 17) to cooking juices after cooking and removing fish. Add ¼ cup minced mushrooms and 1 teaspoon bread crumbs. Heat until foaming. Pour this foaming sauce over cooked fish. Sprinkle with warmed capers and serve with lemon wedges,

Tuna see Mackerel

Whitefish

GRAYLING
CHUB
LAKE HERRING

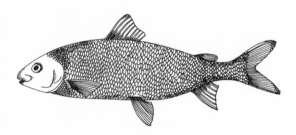

Whitefish is the common name for freshwater fish of the family *Coregonidae*. At one time whitefish was classified in the family *Salmonidae*, which includes salmon and trout, because of their similar characteristics. The whitefish family includes the chub, grayling, and lake herring. The large California whitefish is a completely different family and should not be confused with the *Coregonidae*.

Whitefish are becoming rare due to overfishing and to the parasitic lamprey eel, which attaches itself to the flesh of the fish and feeds on it. Whitefish do not eat other fish. The flesh of the whitefish is lean and mild-flavored.

WHITEFISH

The whitefish has large, smooth, stiff scales and weak jaws with very few teeth. Its white fins give it its name. The body coloring varies with locality but pale green and bluish-silver are the most common. A silver variety with a gray back is also seen at the market. A fat-fleshed fish, it averages from 2 to 6 pounds.

CHUB

Chub is a very popular fish and has the reputation for superior flavor. There are seven or more species, but only one, the blackfin, is marketed fresh. The average weight is 6 ounces. It is a very thin fish with soft flesh.

GRAYLING

Grayling has large scales and a small mouth with a very high dorsal fin. The grayling is magnificently colored in hues of silver, violet, gold, olive, brown, and blue with spotted flanks. The average weight is 1 pound, but occasionally it weighs as much as 4 pounds. The flesh of fresh grayling has the taste and aroma of fresh thyme.

LAKE HERRING (ciscoes)

Lake herring are not related to the sea herring. They are elliptical in shape with compressed bodies, their color an iridescent blue-black without any markings. They have tiny teeth on the tongue. The flesh is rich and oily but delicate in flavor; a few species, however, are lean-fleshed. The average weight is 5 to 6 ounces but they rarely weigh more than 1 pound.

LOCATION

Whitefish are found in the Great Lakes and other lakes in the United States and Canada.

MARKET

The whitefish family is available year round. They are marketed fresh, smoked, kippered, salted, and as fillets. They are very popular frozen. Most are purchased smoked. The lake herring can be found salted. The peak of the season for fresh lake herring is April and May. Whitefish roe is delicious, but rare.

COOKING

- Fillets can be cooked in any way desired, served with any sauce or butter.
- Excellent in chowders.
- Whitefish roe can be sautéed or salted and used as caviar.
- Small fish can be pan fried or oven fried: serve with tartar sauce, or lemon butter.
- Poach whitefish in a milk-and-water court bouillon: serve with oyster sauce, shrimp sauce, or Hollandaise sauce.
- Serve baked with a tangy sauce to accentuate the savory flavor.
- Lake herring should not be drawn or washed. Just wipe with a damp cloth. Leave the head intact and deep-fat fry to a golden brown.
- Because chub is so bony, it should be scored (make small cuts through the skin only) several times on each side to soften the bones and then deep fried. The bones can usually be eaten if prepared properly.

FRIED LAKE HERRING

---

2 pounds lake herring
1 cup flour
  Salt and pepper to taste
1 cup oil

2 tablespoons fresh parsley, chopped, or 1 tablespoon dried parsley flakes
  Lemon wedges

Put flour into a plastic bag and season with salt and pepper. Place herring into the bag, 1 or 2 at a time, and shake bag gently until fish is coated with flour. Heat oil. Deep fry for about 5 minutes. Garnish cooked fish with parsley and lemon wedges.

Index

[Page numbers in italics (*82*) refer to locations of recipes.]

About the Author

Shirley Ross is a home, health, and food expert, and the author of several books, including *The Interior Ecology Cookbook, Nature's Drinks*, and the extremely popular *First Aid for House Plants*. She has tested each recipe and technique for *The Seafood Book* in her New York apartment.

Catalog

If you are interested in a list of fine Paperback
books, covering a wide range of subjects
and interests, send your name and address,
requesting your free catalog, to:

McGraw-Hill Paperbacks
1221 Avenue of Americas
New York, N.Y. 10020